THE BELIEVER'S SECRET OF HOLINESS

THE BELIEVER'S SECRET OF HOLINESS

Andrew Murray

BETHANY HOUSE PUBLISHERS

MINNEAPOLIS, MINNESOTA 55438

A Division of Bethany Fellowship, Inc.

Formerly published under the title *Holy in Christ*.
This edition newly edited.

Copyright © 1984
Bethany House Publishers
All Rights Reserved

Published by Bethany House Publishers
A Division of Bethany Fellowship, Inc.
6820 Auto Club Road, Minneapolis, Minnesota 55438

Printed in the United States of America

Library of Congress Cataloging in Publication Data

Murray, Andrew, 1828–1917.
    The believer's secret of holiness.

    "Formerly titled Holy in Christ"—Verso t.p.
    1. Holiness. I. Title.
BT767.M95   1984   234'.8   84–2973
ISBN 0–87123–432–7 (pbk.)

The Author

ANDREW MURRAY was born in South Africa in 1828. After receiving his education in Scotland and Holland, he returned to that land and spent many years there as both pastor and missionary. He was a staunch advocate of biblical Christianity. He is best known for his many devotional books.

Other Books by Andrew Murray

Preface

No word in Scripture is more distinctly divine in its origin and meaning than the word holy. No other word leads us higher into the mystery of Deity nor deeper into the privilege and blessedness of God's children. And yet few Christians have ever studied or fully comprehended the word.

Many praise God that during the past twenty years the watchword *Be Holy* has spread through many a church and Christian circle with deeper earnestness than ever before. Books and magazines, conventions and conferences, the testimonies and lives of believers, display many signs that what is called the holiness movement is a reality.

But so much is still lacking! Multitudes of believing Christians have only the vaguest concept of what holiness is! Even among those who seek to know, few have learned to come to God's Word and to God himself to be taught—He alone can reveal this part of the mystery of Christ and of himself! To many, holiness has simply been a general expression for the Christian life in its more earnest form, without much thought of all that the term really means.

In writing this book, my object has been to discover in what sense God uses the word so that it may mean to us what it means to Him. I have tried to trace the word through some of the most important passages of Scripture where it occurs, to learn there what God's holiness is and what ours is to be, and to find the way by which we attain it. Especially, I wanted to point out how many, how varied are the elements that make up true holiness as the divine expression of the Christian life in all its fullness and perfection. At the same time I continually tried to emphasize the wonderful unity and simplicity there is in holiness as centered in the person of Jesus. As I proceeded in my work, I felt ever more deeply what an awesome task I had undertaken in offering to guide others even if only into the outer courts of the holy place of the Most High. But the very difficulty of the task convinced me how much it was needed.

To some, I am afraid this book may be a disappointment. They have heard that the entrance to the life of holiness is often only a step. They know about believers who told of the blessed change that came over their lives since they found the wonderful secret of holiness by faith. Now they are seeking for this secret. They cannot understand that the secret comes not to those who seek it, but only to those who seek Jesus. They want to have a book in which all they need to know of holiness and the way it is obtained is in a few simple lessons—easy to learn, to remember and to practice. This they will not find.

There is such a thing as a Pentecost still for the disciples of Jesus; but it comes to him who has forsaken all to follow Jesus only, and in following fully has allowed the Master to reprove and instruct him. There are often very blessed revelations of Christ, as a Savior from sin, both in the secret prayer room and in the meetings of the saints; but these revelations are given to those for whom they have been prepared and who have been prepared to receive. Let all learn to trust in Jesus, and rejoice in Him, even though their experience be not what they would wish. He will make us holy. But whether we have entered the blessed life of faith in Jesus as our sanctification or are still longing for it from afar, we all need one thing—the simple, believing, and obedient acceptance of each word that our God has spoken.

It has been my earnest desire that I might be a helper of the faith of my brethren in seeking to trace with them the wondrous revelation of God's holiness through the ages as recorded in His blessed Word. It has been my continual prayer that God might use what is written to increase in His children the conviction that we must be holy, the knowledge of how we are to be holy, the joy that we may be holy, the faith that we can be holy. And may He stir us all to cry day and night to Him for a visitation of the Spirit and the power of holiness upon all His people, that the name of Christian and of saint may be synonymous, and every believer be a vessel made holy and meet for the Master's use.

Andrew Murray
Wellington, South Africa
November 16, 1887

Contents

CHAPTER ONE

God's Call to Holiness

"But as he which hath called you is holy, so be ye holy in all manner of conversation; because it is written, Be ye holy; for I am holy" (1 Pet. 1:15, 16).

The call of God is the manifestation in time of His purpose in eternity: "Whom he predestinated, them he also called." Believers are "the called according to his purpose." In His call He reveals to us what His thoughts and His will concerning us are, and what the life is to which He invites us. In His call He makes clear to us what the hope of our calling is; as we spiritually apprehend and enter into this, our life on earth will be the reflection of His purpose for us in eternity.

Scripture uses more than one word to indicate the object or aim of our calling, but none more frequently than what Peter speaks of here—God has called us to be holy as He is holy. Paul addresses believers twice as "called to be saints [holy]" (Rom. 1:7; 1 Cor. 1:2). "God hath not called us," he says, "unto uncleanness, but unto holiness" (1 Thess. 4:7). When he writes, "The very God of peace sanctify you wholly," he adds, "Faithful is he that calleth you, who also will do it" (1 Thess. 5:24). The calling itself is spoken of as "a holy calling." The eternal purpose, of which the calling is the outcome, is also continually connected with holiness as its aim. "He hath chosen us in him . . . that we should be holy and without blame" (Eph. 1:4). "God hath from the beginning

13

chosen you to salvation through sanctification" (2 Thess. 2:13). "Elect according to the foreknowledge of the Father, through sanctification of the Spirit" (1 Pet. 1:2). The call is the unveiling of the purpose that the Father from eternity had set His heart upon: that we should be holy.

Without doubt, to know aright what God has called us to is of infinite importance. To misunderstand here could be fatal. That God calls you to salvation or to happiness, to receive pardon or to obtain heaven, you may have heard. But have you ever noticed that all these were subordinate to His main purpose? It was to "salvation through sanctification," it was to holiness first and foremost, as the element in which salvation and heaven are to be found. The complaints of many Christians as to lack of joy and strength, as to failure and lack of growth, are due to this—the place God gave holiness in His call they have not given to it in their response. God and they have never yet come to an agreement on this.

No wonder that Paul, in the chapter in which he had spoken to the Ephesians about being "chosen to be holy," prays for the spirit of wisdom and revelation in the knowledge of God to be given to each believer, that he might know "the hope of his calling" (1:17, 18). Let all of us who now see to what we are called pray this prayer and ask God to show us that, just as He who hath called us is himself holy, so we are to be. Our calling, before and above everything else, is to holiness. Let us ask Him to show us what holiness is, His first and then ours; to show us how He has set His heart upon that as the one thing He wants to see in us, as being His own image and likeness; to show us too the unutterable blessedness and glory of sharing with Christ in His holiness. Oh, that God by His Spirit would teach us all that this calling means! We can easily conceive what a mighty influence it would exert.

"Like as he which called you is holy, be ye yourselves also holy." This call of God shows us the true motive behind His command: "Be ye holy, for I am holy." It is as if God said, "Holiness is my blessedness and my glory: without this you cannot see me or enjoy me; there is nothing higher to be conceived; I invite you to share with me in it; I invite you to likeness to myself. Does this attract you and move you deeply—the hope of being partakers of my holiness? I have nothing better to offer—I offer you myself: 'Be holy, for I am holy.' " Shall we not cry earnestly to God to show us the glory of His holiness, that our souls may be made willing to give everything in response to this wondrous call?

His call also shows the nature of true holiness. "Like as he is holy, so be ye also holy." To be holy is to be Godlike, to have a disposition, a will, a character like God. The thought almost looks like blasphemy until we listen again, "He hath chosen us in Christ to be holy." In Christ the holiness of God appeared in a human life: in Christ's example, in His mind and Spirit, we have the holiness of the Invisible One translated into the forms of human life and conduct. To be Christlike is to be Godlike; to be Christlike is to be holy as God is holy.

The call equally reveals the power of holiness. "There is none holy but the Lord"; there is no holiness but what He has, or rather what He is and gives. The quality is not something we do or attain: it is the communication of the divine life, the inbreathing of the divine nature, the power of the divine presence resting on us. And our power to become holy is to be found in the call of God: the Holy One calls us to himself that He may make us holy in possessing himself. He not only says "I am holy," but "I am the Lord, who makes holy." Because the call comes from the God of infinite power and love, we may have the confidence: we can be holy.

The call no less reveals the standard of holiness. "Like the Holy One who called you, be ye yourselves also holy."* There is not one standard for God and another for man. The nature of light is the same, whether we see it in the sun or in a candle; the nature of holiness remains unchanged, whether it be God or man in whom it dwells. The Lord Jesus could say nothing less than, "Be perfect, even as your Father in heaven is perfect." When God calls us to holiness, He calls us to himself and His own life. The more carefully we listen to the voice, and let it sink into our hearts, the more will all human standards fall away and only the words be heard, Holy, as I am holy.

The call shows us the path of holiness. The calling of God is one of mighty efficacy, an effectual calling. Listen to Him

---

*As in margin, ASV.

and with divine power the call will work what it offers. He calls the things that are not as though they were. His call gives life to the dead and holiness to those whom He has made alive. He calls us to listen as He speaks of His holiness, and of ours like His. He calls us to himself, to study, to fear, to love, to claim His holiness. He calls us to Christ, in whom divine holiness became human holiness, to see and admire, to desire and accept what is all for us. He calls us to the indwelling and the teaching of the Spirit of holiness, to yield ourselves that He may bring home to us and breathe within us what is ours in Christ. Believer, listen to God calling you to holiness; come and learn what His holiness is, and what yours is and what it must be.

Be silent and listen. When God called Abraham, he answered, "Here am I." When God called Moses from the bush, he answered, "Here am I," and he hid his face, for he was afraid to look upon God. God is calling you to himself the Holy One that He may make you holy. Let your whole soul answer, "Here am I, Lord! Speak, Lord! Show yourself, Lord!" As you listen, the voice will sound ever deeper and ever stiller: "Be holy, as I am holy. Be holy, for I am holy." You will hear a voice coming out of the great eternity, from the council chamber of redemption, and as you catch its distant whisper, it will be, "Be holy, I am holy." You will hear a voice from Paradise, the Creator making the seventh day holy for man whom He had created, and saying, "Be holy." You will hear the voice from Sinai, amid thunderings and lightnings, and still it is, "Be holy, as I am holy." You will hear a voice from Calvary, and there above all it is, "Be holy, for I am holy."

Child of God, have you ever heard this call from God? Must we not confess that happiness has been to us more than holiness, salvation more than sanctification? But it is not too late to redeem the error. Listen to the voice that calls, draw nigh, and find out what holiness is, or rather, find out and know Him the Holy One. If the first approach to Him fills us with shame and confusion, makes us fear and shrink back, let us still listen to the voice and call, "Be holy, as I am holy." "Faithful is he which calleth, who also will do it." All our fears and questions will be met by this One who has revealed His holiness with one purpose in view: that we might share it with Him. As we yield ourselves in deep stillness of soul to listen to the holy voice that calls us, it will waken within us new desire and strong faith, and the most precious of all promises will be to us this word of divine command: "Be holy, for I am holy."

Prayer

O Lord, the only Holy One, you have called us to be holy, even as you are holy! Lord, how can we, unless you reveal to us your holiness? Show us how you are holy, how holy you are, what your holiness is, that we may know how we are to be holy and how holy we are to be. And when the sight of you only shows us the more how unholy we are, teach us that you make those partakers of your own holiness who come to you for it.

O God, we come to you, the Holy One. It is in knowing and finding and having yourself that the soul finds holiness. We come to beseech you to burn into our heart that the one object of your calling us and of our coming to you is holiness. You would have us be like yourself, partakers of your holiness. If ever our heart fears that this is too high to attain or rests content with a salvation less than holiness, Blessed God, let us hear your voice calling again, "Be holy, I am holy." Let that call be our motive and our strength, because faithful is He that calleth, who also will do it. Let that call mark our standard and our path. Let our life be such as you are able to make it.

Holy Father, I bow in lowly worship and silence before you. Let your voice sound in the depths of my heart, calling me, "Be holy, as I am holy." Amen.

Personal Application

1. Let me press it upon every reader of this book, that if it is to help him in the pursuit of holiness, he must begin with God himself. You must go to Him who calls you. It is only in the personal revelation of God to you as He speaks, "I am holy," that the command "Be ye holy" can have life or power.

2. Remember, as a believer, you have already accepted God's call, even though you did not fully understand it. Let

it be a settled matter, that whatever you see to be the meaning of the call, you will at once accept and carry out. If God calls me to be holy, holy I will be.

3. Take fast hold of the word: "The God of peace sanctify you wholly: faithful is he which calleth you, who also will do it." In that faith listen to God calling you.

4. Do be still now and listen to your Father calling you. Ask for and count upon the Holy Spirit, the Spirit of holiness, to open your heart to understand this holy calling. And then speak out the answer you have to give to this call.

CHAPTER TWO

God's Provision for Holiness

"To them that are [sanctified] in Christ Jesus, called to be saints [holy ones]" (1 Cor. 1:2).

". . . to all the saints [holy ones] in Christ Jesus which are at Philippi. . . . Salute every saint [holy one] in Christ Jesus"* (Phil. 1:1, 4:21).

Holy and *in Christ* are perhaps the most wonderful words of all the Bible.

Holy is the word of unfathomable meaning, which even seraphs utter with veiled faces. *Holy* is the word in which all God's perfections center, and of which His glory is but the streaming forth. *Holy* is the word which reveals the purpose with which God from eternity thought of man, and foretells man's highest glory in the coming eternity—to be partaker of God's holiness!

In Christ—here all the wisdom and love of God are unveiled: the Father giving His Son to be one with us; the Son

---

*One disadvantage in English is that some synonyms are derived from Saxon and others from Latin. Sometimes in translation of the Bible two different words may be used for what is expressed by only one term in the original. This is the case with the words *holy, holiness, hallow, saint, sanctify,* and *sanctification.* When God or Christ is called the Holy One, the word in Hebrew and Greek is exactly the same that is used when the believer is called a saint: he too is a holy one. So the three words *hallow, keep holy, sanctify,* all represent but one term in the original, of which the real meaning is to make holy.

19

dying on the cross to make us one with Him; the Holy Spirit of the Father dwelling in us to establish and maintain that union! *In Christ*—what a summary of what redemption has done, and of the inconceivably blessed life in which the child of God is permitted to dwell. *In Christ* is the one lesson we have to study on earth, God's one answer to all our needs and prayers, and the guarantee and foretaste of eternal glory.

What wealth of meaning and blessing when the words are combined: holy in Christ. Here is God's provision for our holiness, God's response to our question, How can we be holy? When we hear the call, Be ye holy, even as I am holy, it seems as if there is, and ever must be, a great gulf between the holiness of God and man. But *in Christ* is the bridge that spans the gulf—or better still—His fullness has filled it up.

In Christ God and man meet. There the holiness of God has found us and made us its own, has become human and can indeed become our very own. To the anxious cries and the heart-yearnings of thousands of thirsty souls who have believed in Jesus and yet know not how to be holy, here is God's answer: *Ye are holy in Christ Jesus*. Only listen to these words and believe. Repeat them, even a thousand times, until God's light shines, until your heart is filled with joy and love and the words echo back: Now I see it. I *am* holy in Christ—made holy in Christ Jesus!

As we study these wonderful words, remember that only God himself can reveal to us what holiness truly is. Let us fear our own thoughts and crucify our own wisdom. Let us yield ourselves to receive in the power of the life of God himself, working in us by the Holy Spirit that which is deeper and truer than the mind can fathom—Christ himself as our holiness. Depending upon the teaching of the Spirit of holiness, let us simply accept what Scripture sets before us. The revelation of the Holy One of old was a very slow and gradual one, so now let us, step by step, patiently follow the path of the shining light through the Word. More and more it will shine unto the perfect day.

First we shall have to study the word *holy* in the Old Testament. In Israel as the holy people, the type of us who now are holy in Christ, we shall see with what fullness of symbol God sought to work into the very constitution of the people an understanding of what He would have them be. In the law we shall see how *holy* is the great key word of the redemption which it was meant to serve and prepare for. In the prophets we see the holiness of God revealed as the source from which the coming redemption would spring. They speak not so much of holiness as of the Holy One who, in redeeming love and saving righteousness, would make himself known as the God of His people.

When the depths of meaning in the word begin to open, and the deep need of its blessing is shown in the Old Testament, we must come to the New to find how that need was fulfilled. In Christ, the Holy One of God, divine holiness will be found in human life and human nature. In Him a will—truly human—is being made perfect and through obedience is developing into complete union with the holy will of God. In His sacrifice on the cross, that holy nature yielded itself to death, so that like seed corn, through death it might live again and reproduce itself in us.

The Spirit of God's holiness is given from the throne and represents, reveals and communicates the unseen Christ. In this gift the holy life of Christ descends and takes possession of His people, and they become one with Him. Just as the Old Testament had no higher word than *holy*, the New has none deeper than this, *in Christ*. Being in Him, abiding in Him, being rooted in Him, growing up in Him and into Him in all things are all divine expressions in which the wonderful and complete oneness between us and our Savior are brought as near to us as possible through human language.

The Old Testament taught us what *holy* means. The New what *in Christ* means. In the Word of God, that unites the two expressions, we have the most complete summary of the great redemption that God's love has provided. The everlasting certainty, the wonderful sufficiency, the infinite efficacy of the holiness that God has prepared for us in His Son are all revealed in this blessed, *Holy in Christ*.

"The holy ones in Christ Jesus!" As believers such is the name which we bear in Scripture, in the language of the Holy Spirit. That we are holy in Christ is no mere statement of doctrine. It is no deep theological discussion to which we are invited, but rather, out of the depths of God's loving heart, there comes a voice addressing His beloved children in this way. It is the name by which the Father calls His children.

That name tells us of God's provision for our being holy. It is the revelation of what God has given us and what we already are, of what God waits to work in us, and what can be ours in personal practical possession. That name, gratefully accepted, joyfully confessed, trustfully pleaded, will be the pledge and the power of our attainment of the holiness to which we have been called.

We shall find that all our study and all God's teaching will be comprised in three great lessons. The first a revelation, "I am holy"; the second a command, "Be ye holy"; the third a gift, the link between the two, "Ye are holy in Christ."

First comes the revelation, "I am holy." Our study must be on bended knee, in the spirit of worship and deep humility. If we are to know what *holy* is, God must reveal himself to us. The deep unholiness of our nature and all that is of that nature must be shown to us. Together with Moses and Isaiah, as the Holy One reveals himself to them, we must fear and tremble. We must confess how utterly unfit we are for the revelation or the fellowship without the cleansing of fire. Conscious of our utter impotence to know God through our own wisdom or understanding, our souls must in contrition, brokenness from ourselves and our power or efforts, yield to God's Spirit, the Spirit of holiness, to reveal God as the Holy One. And as we begin to know Him in His infinite righteousness, in His fiery burning zeal against all that is sin, and His infinite self-sacrificing love to free the sinner from his sin, and to bring him to His own perfection, we shall learn to wonder at and worship this glorious God, to feel and deplore our terrible unlikeness to Him, to long and cry for some share in the divine beauty and blessedness of this holiness.

And then will come with new meaning the command, "Be holy, as I am holy." You who profess to obey the commands of your God, give this all-surpassing and all-including command that first place in your heart and life which it claims. Be holy with the likeness of God's holiness. Be holy as He is holy. Perhaps the more you meditate and study, the less you can grasp this infinite holiness. Perhaps the more you at moments grasp of it, the more you despair of a holiness so divine. Then remember that such breaking down and such despair is just what the command was meant to work. Learn to cease from your own wisdom as well as your own goodness.

Draw near in poverty of spirit to let the Holy One show you how utterly above human knowledge or human power is the holiness He demands. To the soul that ceases from self and has no confidence in the flesh, He will show and give the holiness He calls us to.

To such the great gift of holiness in Christ becomes intelligible and acceptable. Christ brings the holiness of God closer by showing it in human conduct and relationships. He brings it within reach by removing the barrier between it and us, between God and us. He brings it nigh, because He makes us one with himself. "Holy in Christ": our holiness is bestowed by God, held for us, communicated to us, working mightily in us because we are in *Christ*. That wonderful *in* shows our very life rooted in the life of Christ. That holy Son and Servant of the Father, beautiful in His life of love and obedience on earth, sanctifying himself for us—that life of Christ is the ground in which I am planted and rooted, the soil from which I draw as my nourishment its every quality and its very nature. How that word sheds its light both on the revelation, "I am holy," and on the command, "Be ye holy, as I am," and binds them into one! In Christ I see what God's holiness is, and what my holiness is. In Him both are one, and both are mine. In Him I am holy. Abiding and growing up in Him, I can be holy in all manner of living, just as God is holy.

Prayer

O Most Holy God, we beseech you to reveal to your children what it means that you have not only called them to holiness, but even called them by this name, "the holy ones in Christ Jesus." Oh, that every child of yours might know that he bears this name, might know what it means, and what power there is in it to change him into what it calls him. Holy Lord God! oh, that the time of your visitation might come soon and each child of yours on earth be known as a holy one!

To this end we pray for you to reveal to your saints what your holiness is. Teach us to worship and to wait until you have spoken to our souls with divine power your word, "I am holy." May it search out and convict us of our unholiness!

Reveal to us, we pray, that just as you are holy and like a consuming fire, so also is your command in its determined and uncompromising purpose to have us holy. O God, let your voice sound through the depth of our being, with a power from which there is no escape: Be holy, be holy.

So let us, between your infinite holiness on the one hand and our unholiness on the other, be driven and be drawn to accept Christ as our sanctification, to abide in Him as our life and our power to be what you would have us be—"holy in Christ Jesus."

Father, let your Spirit make this precious word life and truth within us. Amen.

Personal Application

1. You are entering anew on the study of a divine mystery. "Trust not to your own understanding"; wait for the teaching of the Spirit of truth.

2. In Christ. A commentator says, "The phrase denotes two moral facts: first, the act of faith whereby a man lays hold of Christ; second, the community of life with Him contracted by means of this faith." There is still another fact, the greatest of all: it is by an act of divine power that I am in Christ and am kept in Him. It is this I want to realize: the divineness of my position in Jesus.

3. Grasp the two sides of the truth. You are holy in Christ with a divine holiness. In the faith of that, you are to be holy, to become holy with a human holiness, the divine holiness manifest in all the conduct of a human life.

4. This Christ is a living person, a loving Savior: how He will delight to get complete possession, and do all the work in you! Keep hold of this as we go along: you have a claim on Christ, on His love and power, to make you holy. As His redeemed one, you are at this moment, whatever and wherever you be, in Him. His holy presence and love are around you. You are in Him, in the enclosure of that tender love, which ever encircles you with His holy presence. In that presence, accepted and realized, is your holiness.

CHAPTER THREE

Holiness and Creation

"And God blessed the seventh day, and sanctified it, because that in it he had rested from all his work which God created and made" (Gen. 2:3).

In Genesis we have the book of beginnings. To its first three chapters we are especially indebted for a divine light shining on the many questions to which human wisdom never could find an answer. In our search after holiness, we are led thither too. In the whole book of Genesis the word holy occurs only once. But that one time is in such a connection as to open to us the secret spring from which flows all that the Bible has to teach or to give us of this heavenly blessing. The full meaning of the precious word we want to master, of the priceless blessing we want to get possession of, "sanctified in Christ," begins here in what is written of that wondrous act of God by which He closed His creation work and revealed how wonderfully it would be continued and perfected. When God blessed the seventh day and sanctified it, He lifted it above the other days, and set it apart to a work and a revelation of himself, excelling in glory all that had preceded. In this simple expression, Scripture reveals to us the character of God as the Holy One, who makes holy; the way in which He makes holy, by entering in and resting; and the power of blessing with which God's making holy is ever accompanied. These three lessons are of the deepest importance to study well, as containing the root principles of all the Scripture will have to teach us in our pursuit of holiness.

1. God sanctified the Sabbath day. During the previous six days, from the first calling into existence of the heaven and the earth, down to the making of man, the key word was: God created. All at once a new word and a new work of God is introduced: God sanctified. Something higher than creation, that for which creation is to exist, is now to be revealed; God Almighty is now to be known as God Most Holy. Just as the work of creation shows His power without that power being mentioned, so His making holy the seventh day reveals His character as the Holy One. As omnipotence is the chief of His natural attributes, so holiness is the first of His moral attributes. And just as He alone is Creator, so He alone is Sanctifier; to make holy is His work as truly and exclusively as to create. Blessed is the child of God who truly and fully believes this!

God sanctified the Sabbath day. The word can teach us the nature of the work God does when He makes holy. Sanctification in Paradise cannot be essentially different from sanctification in redemption. God had pronounced all His works, and man the chief of them, very good. And yet they were not holy. The six days' work had nothing of defilement or sin, but still it was not holy. The seventh day especially needed to be made holy for the great work of making man—who was already very good—holy. In Exodus, God says distinctly that He sanctified the Sabbath day, with a view to man's sanctification. "That ye may know that I am the Lord that doth sanctify you."

Goodness, innocence, purity, freedom from sin, are not holiness. Goodness is the work of omnipotence, an attribute of nature, as God creates it. Holiness is something infinitely higher. We speak of the holiness of God as His infinite moral perfection; man's moral perfection could only come in the use of his will, freely consenting to and abiding in the will of God. Only in this way could he become holy. The seventh day was made holy by God as a pledge that He would make man holy. In the ages that preceded the seventh day, the creation period, God's power, wisdom, and goodness had been displayed. The age to come, in the seventh-day period, is to be the dispensation of holiness. God made holy the seventh day.

2. God sanctified the Sabbath day, because in it He rested from all His work. This rest was something real. In creation, God had, as it were, gone out of himself to bring forth something new. In resting He now returns from His creating work into himself, to rejoice in His love over the man He has created, and communicate himself to him. This opens up to us the way in which God makes holy. The connection between the resting and making holy was no arbitrary one. The making holy was no afterthought; in the very nature of things it could not be otherwise. He sanctified because He rested in it. He sanctified by resting. As He regards His finished work, especially man, He rejoices in it, and, as we have it in Exodus, "is refreshed." This time of His divine rest is the time in which He will carry on to perfection what He has begun. He will make man, created in His image, in very deed partaker of His highest glory, His holiness.

Where God rests in complacency and love, He makes holy. The presence of God revealing itself, entering in, and taking possession, is what constitutes true holiness. As we go down the ages, studying the progressive unfolding of what holiness is, this truth will continually confront us. In God's indwelling in heaven, in His temple on earth, in His beloved Son, in the person of the believer through the Holy Spirit, everywhere we shall find that holiness is not something that man is or does, but that it always comes where God comes. In the deepest meaning of the words: where God enters to rest, there He sanctifies. When we study the New Testament revelation of the way in which we are to be holy, we shall find this one of our earliest and deepest lessons. As we enter into the rest of God we become partakers of His holiness. "We which have believed do enter into [that] rest"; "He that hath entered into his rest hath himself also rested from his works, as God did from his."

As the soul ceases from its own efforts, and rests in Him who has finished all for us, and will finish all in us, as the soul yields itself in the quiet confidence of true faith to rest in God, it will know what true holiness is. Where the soul enters into the sabbath stillness of perfect trust, God comes to keep His sabbath holy, and the soul where He rests He sanctifies. Whether we speak of His own day, "He sanctified it," or His own people "sanctified in Christ," the secret of holiness is ever the same: "He sanctified because he rested."

3. Then we read, "He blessed and sanctified it." As used in the first chapter and throughout the book of Genesis, the expression "God blessed" is one of great significance. "Be fruitful and multiply" was to Adam, and later to Noah and Abraham, the divine exposition of its meaning. The blessing with which God blessed Adam and Noah and Abraham was that of fruitfulness and increase, the power to reproduce and multiply. When God blessed the seventh day, He so filled it with the living power of His holiness that in it that holiness might increase and reproduce itself in those who, like Him, seek to enter into its rest and sanctify it. The seventh day is that in which we are still living.

Of each of the creation days it is written, up to the last, "There was evening, and there was morning, the sixth day." Of the seventh the record has not yet been made; we are living in it now, God's own day of rest and holiness and blessing. Entering into it in a very special manner, and taking possession of it, as the time for His rejoicing in His creature, and manifesting the fullness of His love in sanctifying man, God has made the dispensation in which we now live one of divine and mighty blessing. At the same time He has taught us what the blessing is. Holiness is blessedness. Fellowship with God in His holy rest is blessedness. And as all God's blessings in Christ have but one fountain, God's holiness, so they all have but one aim, to make us partakers of that holiness. God created and blessed with the creation blessing. God sanctified and blessed with the sabbath blessing of rest in God and holiness in fellowship with Him.

God's finished work of creation was marred by sin, and our fellowship with Him in the blessing of His holy rest was cut off. The finished work of redemption opened for us a truer rest and a surer entrance into the holiness of God. As He rested in His holy day, so He now rests in His holy Son. In Him we now can enter fully into the rest of God. "Made holy in Christ," let us rest in Him. Let us rest, because we see that just as wonderfully as God by His mighty power finished His work of creation, so will He complete and perfect His work of sanctification. Let us yield ourselves to God in Christ, to rest where He rested, to be made holy with His own holiness, and to be blessed with God's own blessing. God the sanctifier is the name now inscribed upon the throne of God the creator. At the threshold of the history of the human race, there shines this word of infinite promise and hope: "God blessed and sanctified the seventh day because in it he rested."

Prayer

Blessed Lord God, I bow before you in lowly worship. I adore you as God the Creator and God the Sanctifier. You have revealed yourself as God Almighty and God Most Holy. I beseech you to teach me to know and to trust you as such.

I humbly ask you for grace to learn and hold fast the deep spiritual truths you have revealed in making holy the Sabbath day. Your purpose in man's creation is to show forth your holiness, and make him partaker of it. Oh, teach me to believe in you as God my Creator and Sanctifier, to believe with my whole heart that the same almighty power which gave the sixth-day blessing of creation, secures to us the seventh-day blessing of sanctification. Your will is our sanctification.

Teach me, Lord, to understand better how this blessing comes. It is where you enter to rest, to refresh and reveal yourself, that you make that place holy. O my God, may my heart be your resting place! In the stillness and confidence of a restful faith, I would rest in you, believing that you do all in me. Let such fellowship with you, and your love and your will be to me the secret of a life of holiness. I ask it in the name of our Lord Jesus, in whom you have sanctified us. Amen.

Personal Application

1. God the Creator is God the Sanctifier. The Omnipotence that did the first work does the second too. I can trust God Almighty to make me holy. God is holy: if God is everything to me, His presence will be my holiness.

2. Rest is ceasing from work, not to work no more, but to begin a new work. God rests and begins at once to make holy that in which He rests. He created by the word of His power; He rests in His love. Creation was the building of the temple; sanctification is the entering in and taking possession. Oh, that wonderful entering into human nature!

3. God rests only in what is restful, wholly at His disposal. It is in the restfulness of faith that we must look to God the Sanctifier; He will come in and keep His holy Sabbath in the restful soul. We rest in God's rest; God rests in our rest.

4. The God that rests in man whom He made, and in resting sanctifies, and in sanctifying blesses: this is our God. Praise and worship Him, and trust Him to do His work.

5. Rest! what a simple word. The rest of God! What an inconceivable *fullness* of life and love in that word. Let us meditate on it and worship before Him until it overshadows us and we enter into it—the rest of God. Rest *belongs to* God: He alone can give it by making us share His own.

CHAPTER FOUR

Holiness and Revelation

"And when the Lord saw that Moses turned aside to see, God called unto him out of the midst of the bush, and said, Moses, Moses. And he said, Here am I. And he said, Draw not nigh hither; put off thy shoes from off thy feet, for the place whereon thou standest is holy ground. . . . And Moses hid his face; for he was afraid to look upon God" (Ex. 3:4–6).

Why was it holy ground? Because God had come there and occupied it. Where God is, there is holiness. It is the presence of God that makes holy. This is the truth we saw in Paradise when man was just created; here, where Scripture uses the word holy for the second time, it is repeated and enforced. A careful study of the word in the light of the burning bush will further open its deep significance. Let us see what the sacred history, what the revelation of God, and what Moses teach us about this holy ground.

1. Note the place this first direct revelation of God to man as the Holy One takes in sacred history. In Paradise we found the word holy used of the seventh day. We found in God's sanctifying the day of rest a promise of a new dispensation— the revelation of the Almighty Creator to be followed by that of the Holy One making holy. But throughout the book of Genesis the word never occurs again; it is as if God's holiness is in abeyance. Only in Exodus, with the calling of Moses, does it appear again. This is a fact of deep import. Just as a parent or teacher seeks, in early childhood, to impress one

lesson at a time, so God deals in the education of the human race.

After having in the flood exhibited His righteous judgment against sin, He calls Abraham to be the father of a chosen people. And as the foundation of all God's dealings with that people, He teaches Abraham and his seed first of all the lesson of childlike trust—trust in Him as the Almighty, with whom nothing is too wonderful, and trust in Him as the Faithful One, whose oath could not be broken. With the growth of Israel to a people we see the revelation advancing to a new stage. The simplicity of childhood gives way to the waywardness of youth, and God must now interfere with the discipline and restriction of law. Having gained a right to a place in their confidence as the God of their fathers, He prepares them for a further revelation. Of the God of Abraham the chief attribute was that He was the Almighty One; of the God of Israel, Jehovah, that He is the Holy One.

What is to be the special mark of the new period that is now about to be inaugurated, and which is introduced by the word holy?

God tells Moses that He is now about to reveal himself in a new character. He had been known to Abraham as God Almighty, the God of Promise (Ex. 6:3). He would now manifest himself as Jehovah, the God of Fulfillment, especially in the redemption and deliverance of His people from the oppression He had foretold to Abraham. God Almighty is the God of Creation. Abraham believed in God, "who quickeneth the dead, and called the things that are not as though they were." Jehovah is the God of redemption and of holiness. With Abraham there was not a word of sin or guilt, and therefore not of redemption or holiness. To Israel the law is to be given to convince of sin and prepare the way for holiness. It is Jehovah, the Holy One of Israel, the Redeemer, who now appears. And it is the presence of this Holy One that makes the ground holy.

2. And how does this Presence reveal itself? In the burning bush God makes himself known as dwelling in the midst of the fire. Elsewhere in Scripture the connection between fire and the holiness of God is clearly expressed: "The light of Israel shall be for a fire, and the Holy One for a flame."

The nature of fire may be either beneficent or destructive. The sun, the great central fire, may give life and fruitfulness or may scorch to death. All depends upon occupying the right position, upon the relation in which we stand to it. And so wherever God the Holy One reveals himself, we shall find the two sides together: God's holiness as judgment against sin, destroying the sinner who remains in it, and as mercy freeing His people from it. Judgment and mercy ever go together. Of the elements of nature, there is none of such spiritual and mighty energy as fire. What it consumes it takes and changes into its own spiritual nature, rejecting as smoke and ashes what cannot be assimilated. And so the holiness of God is that infinite perfection by which He keeps himself free from all that is not divine, and yet has fellowship with the creature and takes it up into union with himself, destroying and casting out all that will not yield itself to Him.

It is thus as One who dwells in the fire, who is a fire, that God reveals himself at the opening of this new redemption period. With Abraham and the patriarchs, as we have said, there had been little teaching about sin or redemption; the nearness and friendship of God had been revealed. Now the law will be given, sin will be made manifest, the distance from God will be felt in order that man, in learning to know himself and his sinfulness, may learn to know and long for God to make him holy. In all God's revelation of himself, we shall find the combination of the two elements, the one repelling, the other attracting. In His house He will dwell in the midst of Israel, and yet it will be in the awful unapproachable solitude and darkness of the holiest of all within the veil. He will come near to them, and yet keep them at a distance. As we study the holiness of God, we shall see in increasing clearness how, like fire, it repels and attracts, how it combines into one His infinite distance and His infinite nearness.

3. But the distance will be that which comes out first and most strongly. This we see in Moses. He hid his face, for He feared to look upon God. The first impression which God's holiness produces is that of fear and awe. Until man, both as a creature and a sinner, learns how high God is above him, how different and distant he is from God, the holiness of God will have little real value or attraction. Moses hiding

his face shows us the effect of the drawing near of the Holy One, and the path to His further revelation.

How distinctly this comes out in God's own words: "Draw not nigh hither; put off thy shoes from off thy feet." Yes, God had drawn nigh, but Moses may not. God comes near: man must stand back. In the same breath God says, Draw nigh, and Draw not nigh. There can be no knowledge of God or nearness to Him, where we have not first heard His "draw not nigh." The sense of sin, of unfitness for God's presence, is the groundwork of true knowledge or worship of Him as the Holy One. "Put off thy shoes from off thy feet." Shoes are the means of contact with the world, the aids through which the flesh or nature does its will, moves about and does its work. In standing upon holy ground, all this must be put away. It is with naked feet, naked and stripped of every covering, that man must bow before a holy God. Our utter unfitness to draw nigh or have any dealings with the Holy One is the very first lesson we have to learn if ever we are to participate in His holiness. That *put off* must exercise its condemning power through our whole being, until we come to realize the full extent of its meaning in the great, "Put off the old man; put on the Lord Jesus," and what "the putting off of the body of the flesh, in the circumcision of Christ," is. Yes, all that is of nature and the flesh, all that is of our own doing or willing or working—our very life—must be put off and given unto the death if God, as the Holy One, is to make himself known to us.

We have seen before that holiness is more than goodness or freedom from sin; even unfallen nature is not holy. Holiness is that awful glory by which divinity is separated from all that is created. Therefore even the seraphs veil their faces with their wings when they sing the thrice holy. But—when the distance and the difference is not that of the creature only but of the sinner, who can express, who can realize, the humiliation, the fear, the shame with which we ought to bow before the voice of the Holy One?

Alas! This is one of the most terrible effects of sin—that it blinds us. We know not how unholy, how abominable, sin and the sinful nature are in God's sight. We have lost the power of recognizing the holiness of God. In heathen philosophy there is no idea of the word holiness as expressive of the moral character of its gods. In losing the light of the glory of God, we have lost the power of knowing what sin is.

So God's first work in drawing nigh to us is to make us feel that we may not draw near as we are; that there will have to be a very real and a very solemn stripping—and even giving up to the death—of all that appears most lawful and most needful. Not only our shoes are soiled with contact with this unholy earth; even our face must be covered and our eyes closed, as a token that the eyes of our heart, all our human wisdom and understanding, are incapable of beholding the Holy One. The first lesson in the school of personal holiness is to fear and hide our face before the holiness of God. "Thus saith the high and lofty One, whose name is Holy, I dwell in the high and holy place, and with him that is of a contrite and humble spirit." Contrition, brokenness of spirit, fear and trembling are God's first demand from those who would see His holiness.

Moses was to be the first preacher of the holiness of God. Of the full communication of God's holiness to us in Christ, His first revelation to Moses was the type and the pledge. From Moses' lips the people of Israel, and later from his pen the Church of Christ, were to receive the message, "Be holy. I am holy. I make holy." His preparation for being the messenger of the Holy One was here, where he hid his face because he was afraid to look upon God. It is with the face in the dust, it is in the putting off not only of the shoes but of all that has been in contact with the world and self and sin that the soul draws nigh to the fire in which God dwells, and which burns but does not consume. Oh, that every believer, who seeks to witness for God as the Holy One, might thus learn how the fulfillment of the type of the burning bush is the Crucified Christ, and how, as we die with Him, we receive that baptism of fire, which reveals in each of us what it means: the Holy One dwelling in a burning bush. Only so can we learn what it is to be holy, as He is holy.

Prayer

Most Holy God, I have seen you who dwell in the fire. I have heard your voice, Draw not nigh hither; put thy shoes

*off from thy feet. And my soul has feared to look upon God,
the Holy One.*

*And yet, O my God, I must see you! You created me to
bear your likeness. You taught that this likeness is your holiness: "Be holy, as I am holy." O my God, how shall I know
how to be holy unless I may see you, the Holy One? To be holy
I must look upon God.*

*I bless you for the revelation of yourself in the flames of
the thorn-bush, in the fire of the accursed tree. I bow in amaze-
ment and deep abasement at the great sight: your Son in the
weakness of His human nature, in the fire, burning but not
consumed. O my God, in fear and trembling I have yielded
myself as a sinner to die like Him. Oh, let the fire consume
all that is unholy in me! Let me, too, know you as the God
that dwells in the fire, to melt down and purge out and destroy
what is not of you, to save and take up into your own holiness
what is your own.*

*O Holy Lord God, I bow in the dust before this great mys-
tery. Reveal to me your holiness that I too may be its witness
and its messenger on earth. Amen.*

Personal Application

1. Holiness as the fire of God. Praise God that there is a
power that can consume the vile and the dross, a power that
will not leave it undisturbed. "The bush burning but not
consumed" is not only the motto of the Church in time of
persecution; it is the watchword of every soul in God's sanctifying work.

2. There is a new theology which only speaks of the love
of God as seen in the cross. It sees not the glory of His righteousness and His righteous judgment. This is not the God
of Scripture. "Our God is a consuming fire" is New Testament
theology. To "offer service with reverence and awe" is New
Testament religion. In holiness, judgment and mercy meet.

3. Holiness as the fear of God. Hiding the face before God
for fear, not daring to look or speak—this is the beginning
of rest in God. It is not yet the true rest, but on the way to
it. May God give us a deep fear of whatever could grieve or
anger Him. May we have a deep fear of ourselves and all
that is of the old, the condemned nature, lest it rise again.

"The spirit of the fear of the Lord" is the first manifestation of the spirit of holiness, and prepares the way for the joy of holiness. "Walking in the fear of the Lord, and in the comfort of the Holy Ghost"; these are the two sides of the Christian life.

4. The holiness of God was revealed to Moses that he might be its messenger. The Church needs nothing so much today as men and women who can testify for the holiness of God. Will you be one?

Additional Note

The connection between the fear of God and holiness is most intimate. There are some who seek most earnestly for holiness and yet never exhibit it in a light that will attract the world or even believers because this element is wanting. It is the fear of the Lord that works that meekness and gentleness, that deliverance from self-confidence and self-consciousness, which form the true groundwork of a saintly character. The passages of God's Word in which the two words are linked together are well worthy of a careful study.

Who is like unto thee, glorious in holiness, fearful in praises?

In thy fear will I worship towards thy holy temple.

O fear the Lord, ye his holy ones.

O worship the Lord in the beauty of holiness, fear before him, all the earth.

Let them praise thy great and terrible name; holy is he.

The fear of the Lord is the beginning of wisdom; and the knowledge of the Holy One is understanding.

The Lord of hosts, him shall ye sanctify; let him be your fear, and let him be your dread.

Perfecting holiness in the fear of the Lord.

Like as he which called you is holy, be ye yourselves also holy; and if ye call on him as father, pass the time of your sojourning in fear.

And so on through the whole of Scripture, from the Song of Moses on to the Song of the Lamb: "Who shall not fear thee, O Lord! and glorify thy name, for thou only art holy." If we meditate on these passages and yield to their message, what will happen? We will become sensitive and fearful of offending God in any way. Especially will we fear to enter His holy presence with what is human and carnal, with anything of our own wisdom and effort. With deep conviction, we will recognize that this fear of God is the very essence of the holiness we are to follow after.

This fear of God will make us, like Moses, fall down and hide our face in God's presence, and wait for His own Holy Spirit to open in us the eyes, and breathe in us the thoughts and the worship, with which we draw nigh to Him, the Holy One. This holy fear works out that stillness of soul which leads it to rest in God, and opens the way for what we saw in Paradise to be the secret of holiness: God keeping His sabbath and sanctifying the soul in which He rests.

CHAPTER FIVE

Holiness and Redemption

"Sanctify unto me all the firstborn" (Ex. 13:2).
"All the firstborn are mine; for on the day that I smote all the firstborn in the land of Egypt I hallowed [sanctified] unto me all the firstborn in Israel . . . mine shall they be: I am the Lord" (Num. 3:13).
"For I am the Lord that bringeth you up out of the land of Egypt to be your God: ye shall therefore be holy, for I am holy" (Lev. 11:45).
"I have redeemed thee . . . thou art mine" (Isa. 43:1).

At Horeb the first mention of the word holy in the history of fallen man was connected with the inauguration of a new period in the revelation of God, that of redemption. In the Passover we have the first manifestation of what redemption is, and here the more frequent use of the word holy begins. In the feast of unleavened bread we have the symbol of the putting off of the old and the putting on of the new, to which redemption through blood is to lead. Of the seven days we read: "In the first day there shall be an holy convocation, and in the seventh day there shall be an holy convocation"; the meeting of the redeemed people to commemorate its deliverance is a holy gathering; they meet under the covering of their Redeemer, the Holy One. As soon as the people had been redeemed from Egypt, God's very first word to them was, "Sanctify—make holy unto me all the firstborn. . . . It is mine" (see Ex. 13:2). The word reveals how proprietorship is one of the central thoughts both in redemption and in sanctification, the link that binds them together. And though the word is here only used of the firstborn, they are regarded as the type of the whole people.

We know how all growth and organization commence from a center, around which in ever-widening circles the life of the organism spreads. If holiness in the human race is to be true and real, free as that of God, it must be the result of a self-appropriating development. And so the firstborn are sanctified, and afterward the priests in their place, as the type of what the whole people is to be as God's firstborn among the nations, His peculiar treasure, "an holy nation." This idea of proprietorship as related to redemption and sanctification comes out with special clearness when God speaks of the exchange of the priests for the firstborn (Num. 3:12, 13; 8:16, 17): "For they [the Levites] are wholly given unto me. . . . Instead of the firstborn of all the children of Israel have I taken them unto me; for all the firstborn of the children of Israel are mine. . . . On the day that I smote every firstborn in the land of Egypt I sanctified them for myself."

Let us try to realize the relation existing between redemption and holiness. In Paradise we saw what God's sanctifying the seventh day was: He took possession of it, He blessed it, He rested in it and refreshed himself. Where God enters and rests, there is holiness. The more perfectly the object is fitted for Him to enter and dwell, the more perfect the holiness. The seventh day was sanctified as the period for man's sanctification. At the very first step God took to lead him to His holiness—the command not to eat of the tree—man fell. God did not give up His plan, but had now to pursue a different and slower path.

After centuries of slow but needful preparation, He now reveals himself as the Redeemer. A people whom He had chosen and formed for himself, He gives up to oppression and slavery that their hearts may be prepared to long for and welcome a deliverer. In a series of mighty wonders He proves himself the conqueror of their enemies, and then, in the blood of the Paschal Lamb on their doors, teaches them what redemption is, not only from an unjust oppressor here on earth, but from the righteous judgment their sins had deserved. The Passover is to be to them the transition from the seen and temporal to the unseen and spiritual, revealing God not only as the Mighty but as the Holy One, freeing them not only from the house of bondage but the destroying angel.

And having thus redeemed them, He tells them that they are now His own. During their stay at Sinai and in the wilderness, the thought is continually pressed upon them that they are now the Lord's people, whom He has made His own by the strength of His arm that He may make them holy for himself, even as He is holy. The purpose of redemption is possession, and the purpose of possession is likeness to Him who is redeemer and owner. That likeness is holiness.

In regard to this holiness, and the way it is to be attained as the result of redemption, there is more than one lesson the sanctifying of the firstborn will teach us.

First of all, we want to realize how inseparable redemption and holiness are. Neither can exist without the other. Only redemption leads to holiness. If I am seeking holiness, I must abide in the clear and full experience of being a redeemed one, and as such of being owned and possessed by God. Redemption is too often looked at from its negative side as deliverance *from*. Its real glory is the positive element of being redeemed *unto* himself. Full possession of a house means occupation. If I own a house without occupying it, it may be the home of all that is foul and evil. God has redeemed me and made me His own with the view of getting complete possession of me. He says of my soul, "It is mine," and seeks to have His right of ownership acknowledged and made fully manifest. That will be perfect holiness, where God has entered in and taken complete and entire possession. It is redemption that gives God His right and power over me. Redemption sets me free for God now to possess and bless. It is redemption realized and filling my soul that will bring me the assurance and experience of all that His power will work in me. In God, redemption and sanctification are one. The more redemption as a divine reality possesses me, the closer am I linked to the Redeemer God, the Holy One.

Only holiness brings the assurance and enjoyment of redemption. If I am seeking to hold fast redemption on lower ground, I may be deceived. If I have become unwatchful or careless, I should tremble at the very idea of trusting in redemption apart from holiness as its object. To Israel God spake, "I brought you up out of the land of Egypt: therefore ye shall be holy, for I am holy." It is God the Redeemer who

42

made us His own, who calls us, too, to be holy. Let holiness
be to us the most essential, the most precious part of redemption: the yielding of ourselves to Him who has taken us
as His own, and has undertaken to make us His own entirely.

A second lesson suggested is the connection between God's
and man's working in sanctification. To Moses the Lord
speaks, "Sanctify unto me all the firstborn." He afterward
says, "I sanctified all the firstborn for myself." What God does
He does to be carried out and appropriated through us. When
He tells us that we are made holy in Christ Jesus, that we
are His holy ones, He speaks not only of His purpose, but of
what He has really done; we have been sanctified in the one
offering of Christ, and in our being created anew in Him.
But this work has a human side. To us comes the call to be
holy, to follow after holiness, to perfect holiness. God has
made us His own, and allows us to say that we are His, but
He waits for us now to yield Him an enlarged entrance into
the secret places of our inner being, for Him to fill it all with
His fullness. Holiness is not something we bring to God or
do for Him. Holiness is what there is of God in us. God has
made us His own in redemption that He might make himself
our own in sanctification. Our work in becoming holy is the
bringing our whole life, and every part of it, into subjection
to the rule of this holy God, putting every member and every
power upon His altar.

This teaches us the answer to the question as to the connection between the sudden and the gradual in sanctification, between its being a thing once for all complete, and yet
imperfect and needing to be perfected. What God sanctifies
is holy with a divine and perfect holiness as His gift. Man
has to sanctify by acknowledging and maintaining and car-
rying out that holiness in relation to what God has made
holy. God sanctified the Sabbath day. Man has to sanctify it,
that is, to keep it holy. God sanctified the firstborn as His
own: Israel had to sanctify them, and then treat and give
them up to God as holy. God is holy. We are to sanctify Him
in acknowledging and adoring and honoring that holiness.
God has sanctified His great name, His name is Holy. We
sanctify or hallow that name as we fear and trust and use it
as the revelation of His holiness. God sanctified Christ. Christ
sanctified himself, manifesting in His personal will and ac-

tion perfect conformity to the holiness with which God had made Him holy. God has sanctified us in Christ Jesus. We are to be holy by yielding ourselves to the power of that holiness, by acting it out, and manifesting it in all our life and walk. The objective divine gift, bestowed once for all and completely, must be appropriated as a subjective personal possession; we must cleanse ourselves, perfecting holiness. Redeemed unto holiness; just as the two thoughts are linked in the mind and work of God, they must be linked in our heart and life.

When Isaiah announced the second, the true redemption, it was given to him, even more clearly and fully than to Moses, to reveal the name of God as "The Redeemer, the Holy One of Israel." The more we study this name, and hallow it, and worship God by it, the more inseparably will the words become connected, and we shall see that just as the Redeemer is the Holy One, the redeemed are holy ones too. Isaiah says of "the way of holiness," the "redeemed shall walk therein." The redemption that comes out from the holiness of God must lead up into it too. We shall understand that to be redeemed in Christ is to be holy in Christ, and the call of our redeeming God will acquire new meaning: "I am holy: be ye holy."

Prayer

O Lord God, the Holy One of Israel and his Redeemer, I worship before you in deep humility. I confess with shame that I so long followed you more as the Redeemer than as the Holy One. I knew not that it was as the Holy One that you redeemed, that redemption was the outcome and the fruit of your holiness; that a participation in your holiness was its one purpose and its highest beauty. I only thought of being redeemed from bondage and death: like Israel, I understood not that without fellowship and conformity to yourself, redemption would lose its value.

Most holy God! I praise you for the patience with which you bear with the selfishness and the slowness of your redeemed ones. I praise you for the teaching of the Spirit of your holiness leading your saints and me, too, to see how it is your holiness and the call to become partaker of it that gives redemption its value. I praise you that we are redeemed that we

*might belong to you, the Holy One, to be possessed and sanc-
tified by you.*

*O my God, with a love and a joy and a thanksgiving that
cannot be uttered, I praise you for Christ, who has been made
unto us sanctification and redemption! In Him you are my
Redeemer, my Holy One. In Him I am your redeemed, your
holy one. O God, in speechless adoration I fall down to worship the love that passeth knowledge, that hath done this for
us, and to believe that in one who is now before you, holy in
Christ, you will fulfill all your glorious purposes according
to the greatness of your power. Amen.*

Personal Application

1. "Redemption through his blood." The blood we meet
at the threshold of the pathway of holiness. For it is the blood
of the sacrifice which the fire of God consumed and yet could
not consume. That blood has such power of holiness in it that
we read, "Sanctified by his own blood." Always think of holiness, or pray for it, as one redeemed by blood. Live under
the covering of the blood in its daily cleansing power.

2. It is only as we know the holiness of God as fire, and
bow before His righteous judgment, that we can appreciate
the preciousness of the blood or the reality of the redemption.
As long as we only think of the love of God as goodness, we
may aim at being good; faith in God who redeems will waken
in us the need and the joy of being holy in Christ.

3. Have you understood the right of property God has in
what He has redeemed? Have you heard a voice say, "Mine.
Thou art mine"? Ask God very humbly to say it to you. Listen
very gently for it.

4. The holiness of the creature has its origin in the divine
will, in the divine election, redemption, and possession. Give
yourself up to this will of God and rejoice in it.

5. As God created, so He redeemed, to sanctify. Have great
faith in Him for this.

6. Let God have the entire possession and disposal of you.
Holiness is His; our holiness is to let Him, the Holy One, be
all.

CHAPTER SIX

Holiness and Glory

"Who is like unto thee, O Lord, among the gods? who is like thee, glorious in holiness, fearful in praises, doing wonders?

"Thou in thy mercy hast led forth the people which thou hast redeemed: thou hast guided them in thy strength unto thy holy habitation ... [the holy place], O Lord, which thy hands have established" (Ex. 15:11, 13, 17).

These words advance us another step in the revelation of holiness. We have here for the first time holiness predicated of God himself. He is glorious in holiness, and it is to the dwelling place of His holiness that He is guiding His people.

Let us first note the expression used here: glorious in holiness. Throughout Scripture we find the glory and the holiness of God mentioned together. In Ex. 29:43 we read, "And the tabernacle shall be sanctified by my glory," that glory of the Lord of which we afterward read that it filled the house. The glory of an object, of a thing or person, is its intrinsic worth or excellence; to glorify is to remove everything that could hinder the full revelation of that excellence. In the holiness of God His glory is hidden; in the glory of God His holiness is manifested. His glory, the revelation of himself as the Holy One, would make the house holy. In the same way the two are connected in Lev. 10:3, "I will be sanctified in them that come nigh me, and before all the people I will be glorified." The acknowledgment of His holiness in the priests would be the manifestation of His glory to the people.

So, too, in the song of the seraphim (Isa. 6:3), "Holy, holy, holy, is the Lord God of hosts: the whole earth is full of his glory." God is He who dwells in a light that is unapproachable, whom no man has seen or can see. It is the light of the knowledge of the glory of God that He gives into our hearts. The glory is that which can be seen and known of the invisible and unapproachable light; that light itself, and the glorious fire of which that light is the shining out, that light is the holiness of God. Holiness is not so much an attribute of God as the comprehensive summary of all His perfections.

On the shore of the Red Sea Israel praises God: "Who is like unto thee, O Lord among the gods? who is like thee, glorious in holiness?" He is the Incomparable One; there is none like Him. Where has He proved this, and revealed the glory of His holiness?

With Moses in Horeb we saw God's glory in the fire, in its double aspect of salvation and destruction, consuming what could not be purified, purifying what was not consumed. Here, too, in the song of Moses, Israel sings of judgment and of mercy. The pillar of fire and of the cloud came between the camp of the Egyptians and the camp of Israel— a cloud and darkness to the Egyptians, but light by night to God's people. The two thoughts run through the whole song. Following the ascription of holiness (Ex. 15:11), we find the destruction of verse 12: "Thou stretchedst out thy right hand, the earth swallowed them." This is the glory of holiness as judgment and destruction of the enemy.

"Thou in thy mercy hast led forth the people which thou hast redeemed: thou hast guided them in thy strength unto thy holy habitation." This is the glory of holiness in mercy and redemption—a holiness that not only delivers but guides to the habitation of holiness, where the Holy One is to dwell with and in His people. So in the inspiration of the hour of triumph, it is revealed that the great object and fruit of redemption, as worked out by the Holy One, is to be His indwelling; with nothing short of this can the Holy One rest content, or the full glory of His holiness be made manifest.

Observe further, how, as it is in the redemption of His people that God's holiness is revealed, so it is in the song of redemption that the personal ascription of holiness to God is found. We know how in Scripture, after some striking special interposition of God as Redeemer, the special influence of the Spirit is manifested in some song of praise. In these outbursts of enthusiasm, it is remarkable how God is praised as the Holy One. See it in the song of Hannah, "There is none holy as the Lord" (1 Sam. 2:2). The language of the seraphim (Isa. 6) is that of a song of adoration. In the great day of Israel's deliverance the song will be, "The Lord Jehovah is become my strength and song. Sing unto the Lord, for he hath done excellent things. Cry aloud and shout, thou inhabitant of Zion, for great is the Holy One of Israel in the midst of thee." Mary sings, "For he that is mighty hath done great things to me: and holy is his name." The book of Revelation reveals the living creatures giving glory and honor and thanks to Him that sits on the throne; "and they have no rest day and night, saying, Holy, holy, holy is the Lord God, the Almgihty, which was, and which is, and which is to come." And when the song of Moses and of the Lamb is sung by the sea of glass, it will still be, "Who shall not fear, O Lord, and glorify thy name? for thou only art holy." It is in the moments of highest inspiration, under the fullest manifestation of God's redeeming power, that His servants speak of His holiness. In Psalm 97 we read, "Rejoice in the Lord, ye righteous, and give thanks at the remembrance of his holiness." And in Psalm 99 (which, with its thrice-repeated holy, has been called the echo on earth of the Thrice Holy of heaven), we sing—

> Let them praise Thy great and terrible name.
> Holy is He.
>
> Exalt ye the Lord our God,
> and worship at His footstool:
> Holy is He.
>
> Exalt ye the Lord our God,
> and worship at His holy hill:
> For the Lord our God is holy.

Only under the influence of high spiritual elevation and joy can God's holiness be fully apprehended or rightly worshiped. The sentiment that becomes us as we worship the Holy One, that fits us for knowing and worshiping Him aright, is the spirit of praise that sings and shouts for joy in the experience of His full salvation.

But does this contradict the lesson we learned at Horeb, when God said, "Draw not nigh hither: put off thy shoes," and where Moses feared and hid his face? Is not this hiding our face the fitting attitude for us as creatures and sinners? Indeed it is. But the two sentiments are not contradictory; rather they are indispensable to each other. The fear is the preparation for the praise and the glory. Or is it not that same Moses who hid his face and feared to look upon God, who afterward beheld His glory until his own face shone with a brightness that men could not bear to look upon? Is not this song that sings of God as glorious in holiness also the song of Moses who feared and hid his face? Have we not seen, in the fire and in God—especially in His holiness—a twofold aspect: consuming and purifying, repelling and attracting, judging and saving? In each case the latter is not only the accompaniment but also the result of the former.

So we find the deeper the humbling and fear in God's holy presence, the more real and complete the putting off of all that is of self and nature, even to the complete death of the old man and his will, and the more hearty the giving up to be consumed of what is sinful, the deeper and fuller will be the praise and joy with which we daily sing our song of redemption: "Who is like unto thee, O Lord, glorious in holiness, fearful in praises, doing wonders?"

"Glorious in holiness, fearful in praises." The song itself harmonizes the apparently conflicting elements. Yes, I will sing of judgment and of mercy. I will rejoice with trembling as I praise the Holy One. As I look upon the two sides of His holiness, as revealed to the Egyptians and the Israelites, I remember that what was there separated is in me united. By nature I am the Egyptian, an enemy doomed to destruction; by grace, an Israelite chosen for redemption. In me the fire must consume and destroy; only as judgment does its work can mercy fully save. It is only as I tremble before the searching light and the burning fire and the consuming heat of the Holy One, as I yield the Egyptian nature to be judged and condemned and slain, that the Israelite will be redeemed to know aright his God as the God of salvation, and to rejoice in Him.

Blessed be God! the judgment is past. In Christ, the burning bush, the fire of the divine holiness did its double work.

In Him sin was condemned in the flesh, in Him we are free. In giving up His will to the death and doing God's will, Christ sanctified himself, and in that will we are sanctified too. His crucifixion with its judgment of the flesh, His death with its entire putting off of what is of nature, are not only for us, but are really ours, a life and a power working within us by His Spirit. Day by day we abide in Him. Tremblingly but rejoicingly we take our stand in Him, for the power of holiness as judgment to vindicate within us its fierce vengeance against what is sin and flesh, and so to let the power of holiness as redemption accomplish that glorious work that makes us give thanks at the remembrance of His holiness. And so the shout of salvation rings ever deeper, truer, louder through our life, "Who is like unto thee, O Lord, among the gods? Who is like unto thee, glorious in holiness, fearful in praises, doing wonders?"

Prayer

"Who is like unto thee, O Lord, glorious in holiness, fearful in praises, doing wonders?" With my whole heart would I join in this song of redemption and rejoice in you as the God of my salvation.

O my God! let your Spirit, from whom these words of holy joy and triumph came, so reveal within me the great redemption as a personal experience, that my whole life may be one song of trembling and adoring wonder.

I beseech you especially to let my whole heart be filled with yourself, glorious in holiness, fearful in praises, who alone doest wonders. Let the fear of your holiness make me tremble at all there is in me of self and flesh. Lead me in my worship to deny and crucify my own wisdom that the Spirit of your holiness may breathe in me. Let the fear of the Lord give its deep undertone to all my coming into and going out of your holy presence. Prepare me thus to praise without ceasing at the remembrance of your holiness. I would rejoice in you as my Redeemer, my Holy One, with a joy unspeakable and full of glory. As my Redeemer, you make me holy. With my whole heart do I trust you to do it, to sanctify me wholly. I do believe in your promise. I do believe in you, and believing I receive you, the Holy One, my Redeemer.

Who is like unto you, O Lord, glorious in holiness, fearful in praises, doing wonders?

Personal Application

1. God's holiness as glory. God is glorified in the holiness of His people. True holiness always gives glory to God alone. Live to the glory of God: that is holiness. Live a holy life: that will glorify God. To lose sight of self and seek only God's glory is holiness.

2. Our holiness as praise. Praise gives glory to God, and is thus an element of holiness. "Thou art holy, thou that inhabitest the praises of Israel."

3. God's holiness, His holy redeeming love, is cause of unceasing joy and praise. Praise God every day for it. But you cannot do this unless you live in it. As we understand that whatever we see of God's glory is just the outshining of His holiness, may His holiness become so glorious to us that we cannot help rejoicing in it, and in Him the Holy One.

4. The spirit of the fear of the Lord and the spirit of praise may at first sight appear to be at variance. But it is not so. The humility that fears the Holy One will also praise Him: "Ye that fear the Lord: praise the Lord." The lower and more humbly we lie in the fear of God and the fear of self, the more surely will He lift us up in due time to praise Him.

CHAPTER SEVEN

Holiness and Obedience

"Ye have seen what I did unto the Egyptians, and how I bare you on eagles' wings, and brought you unto myself. Now therefore, if ye will obey my voice indeed, and keep my covenant, then ye shall be a peculiar treasure unto me above all people . . . ye shall be unto me . . . an holy nation" (Ex. 19:4–6).

Israel has reached Horeb. The law is to be given and the covenant made. Here are God's first words to the people; He speaks of redemption and its blessing, fellowship with himself: "Ye have seen how I brought you unto myself." He speaks of holiness as His purpose in redemption: "Ye shall be unto me an holy nation." As the link between the two He places obedience: "If ye will indeed obey my voice, ye shall be unto me an holy nation." God's will is the expression of His holiness; as we do His will, we come into contact with His holiness. The link between redemption and holiness is obedience.

This takes us back to what we saw in Paradise. God sanctified the seventh day as the time for sanctifying man. And what was the first thing He did with this purpose? He gave him a commandment. Obedience to that commandment would have opened the door, would have been the entrance, into the holiness of God.

Holiness is a moral attribute, and moral is that which a free will chooses and determines for itself. What God creates and gives is only naturally good; what man wills to have of

51

God and His will, and really appropriates, has moral worth, and leads to holiness.

In creation God manifested His wise and good will. His holy will He speaks in His commands. As that holy will enters man's will and as man's will accepts and unites itself with God's will, he becomes holy. After creation, in the seventh day, God enrolled man in His work of sanctification to make him holy. Obedience is the path to holiness, because it is the path to union with God's holy will. With man unfallen just as with fallen man, in redemption here and in glory above, in all the holy angels and even in Christ the Holy One of God himself, *obedience is the path of holiness*. Obedience itself is not holiness, but as the will opens itself to accept and to do the will of God, God communicates himself and His holiness. To obey His voice is to follow Him as He leads in the way to the full revelation and communication of himself and His blessed nature as the Holy One.

Obedience is not knowledge of the will of God, not even approval, not even the will to do it, but the doing of it. Knowledge and approval and will must all lead to action; the will of God must be done. "If ye indeed obey my voice, ye shall be unto me an holy nation." Here it is not faith, not worship, not profession, that God asks from His people when He speaks of holiness. It is obedience. God's will must be done on earth as in heaven. "Remember, and do all my commandments, and be holy unto your God" (Num. 15:40). "Sanctify yourselves therefore, and be ye holy . . . and ye shall keep my statutes and do them: I am the Lord which sanctify you" (Lev. 20:7, 8). "Therefore shall ye keep my commandments, and do them: I am the Lord . . . I will be hallowed among the children of Israel: I am the Lord which hallow you, that brought you up out of the land of Egypt" (22:31–33).

A moment's reflection makes this clear. A man's work manifests what he is. I may know what is good and yet not approve it. I may approve but still not will it. In a certain sense I may will a thing but even so, may lack the energy or self-sacrifice or power that will arouse me to do that thing. Thinking is easier than willing, and willing is easier than doing. *Action alone* proves whether the object of my interest has complete mastery over me. God wants His will done. This alone is obedience. Only in this way is it seen whether the

whole heart, with all its strength and will, has fully yielded
to the will of God; whether we live His will and are ready at
any sacrifice to make it our own by doing it. God has no other
way for making us holy. "Ye shall keep my statutes and do
them: I am the Lord which make you holy."

To all seekers after holiness this lesson is of deep importance. Obedience is not holiness. Holiness is something far
higher, something that comes from God to us—or rather,
something of God coming into us. But obedience is indispensable to holiness. It cannot exist without it. As your heart
seeks to follow God's Word and looks back in faith to what
God has done in making you holy in Christ; as you look ahead
to what God still will do through His Holy Spirit to fulfill
the promise, "The very God of peace sanctify you wholly,"
never for one moment forget to be obedient.

"If ye shall indeed obey my voice, ye shall be an holy
nation to me." Begin by doing at once whatever appears right
to do. Give up at once whatever conscience tells you is not
according to the will of God. Not only pray for light and
strength, but act. Do what God says. "He that doeth the will
of God is my brother," Jesus says. Every son of God has been
begotten of the will of God; in doing that will he has his life.
To do the Father's will is the meat, the strength, the mark
of every son of God.

Surrender to such a life of simple and entire obedience is
implicit in becoming a Christian. It is sad that too many
Christians, either from lack of correct instruction or from
insufficient attention to the teaching of God's Word, have
never realized the place of supreme importance that obedience takes in the Christian life. They do not know that Christ,
redemption and faith all lead to obedience, because through
that alone is the way to the fellowship of the love, the likeness, and the glory of God. We have all possibly suffered from
ignorance of that fact. In our prayers and striving for perfect
peace and the rest of faith, the abiding joy and increasing
power of the Christian life, a secret something has hindered
the blessing or caused the rapid loss of what had been apprehended. A wrong concept about the absolute necessity of
obedience was probably the cause. *The freeness and mighty
power of grace, from our conversion onwards, moves toward
the object of restoring us to the active obedience and harmony*

*with God's will from which we had fallen through the first
sin in Paradise.* Obedience leads to God and His holiness. In
obedience the will is molded and the character formed, and
an inner man is built up which God can clothe and adorn
with the beauty of holiness.

When a Christian discovers that this has been the missing link, the cause of failure and darkness, he must in a
grand act of surrender, deliberately choose obedience—universal, wholehearted obedience—as the law of his life in the
power of the Holy Spirit. May he make his own the words of
Israel at Sinai, in answer to the message of God we are con-
sidering: "All that the Lord hath spoken, we will do"; "All
that the Lord hath said will we do, and be obedient." What
the law could not do, in that it was weak through the flesh,
God has done by the gift of His Son and Spirit. The lawgiving
of Sinai on tables of stone has been succeeded by the lawgiving of the Spirit on the table of the heart. The Holy Spirit is
the power of obedience, and is so the Spirit of holiness, who,
in obedience, prepares our hearts for being the dwelling of
the Holy One. In this faith, let us yield ourselves to a life of
obedience. It is the New Testament path to the realization
of the promise, "If ye will obey my voice indeed, ye shall be
unto me an holy nation."

We have already seen how holiness in its very nature
assumes the truth of a personal relation to God, His personal
presence. "I have brought you unto myself; if ye obey, ye shall
be unto me an holy nation." As we understand and hold fast
this personal element, obedience will become possible and
will lead to holiness. Mark well God's words: "If ye will obey
my voice, and keep my covenant." The voice is more than a
law or a book; it always implies a living person and communication with him. This is the secret of gospel obedience:
hearing the voice and following the lead of Jesus as a personal friend, a living Savior. It is being led by the Spirit of
God, having Him reveal the presence, the will and the love
of the Father, that will work in us that personal relation
which the New Testament means when it speaks of doing
everything unto the Lord, as pleasing God.

Such obedience is the pathway of holiness. Its every act
is a link to the living God, a surrender of the being for God's
will, for God himself to take possession. In the process of

assimilation, slow but sure, by which the will of God, as the meat of our souls, is accepted into our inmost being, our spiritual nature is strengthened, is spiritualized, growing up into an holy temple in which God can reveal himself and take up His abode.

When God sanctified the seventh day as His period of making holy, He taught us that He could not do it all at once. The revelation and communication of holiness must be gradual, as man is prepared to receive it. God's sanctifying work with each of us, as with the race, needs time. The time it needs and seeks is the life of daily, hourly obedience. All that is spent in self-will, and not in the living relation to the Lord, is lost. But when the heart seeks day by day to hearken to the voice and to obey it, the Holy One himself watches over His words to fulfill them: "Ye shall be unto me an holy nation." In a way of which the soul beforehand can have but little conception, God will overshadow and make His abode in the obedient heart. The habit of always listening for the voice and obeying it will only be the building of the temple: the living God himself, the Holy One, will come to take up His abode. The glory of the Lord will fill the house, and the promise be made true, "I will sanctify it by my glory."

"I brought you unto myself; if ye will obey my voice indeed, ye shall be unto me an holy nation." Seekers after holiness—God has brought you to himself. Now His voice speaks to you all the thoughts of His heart, so that as you take them in and make them your own, and make His will your own by living and doing it, you may enter into the most complete union with Him, the union of will as well as of life, and so become a holy people unto Him. Let obedience, listening to and doing the will of God, be the joy and the glory of your life. It will give you access unto the holiness of God.

Prayer

O my God, you have redeemed me for yourself that you might have me wholly as your own, possessing, filling my inmost being with your own likeness, your perfect will, and the glory of your holiness. And you seek to train me, in the power of a free and loving will, to take your will and make it my own, that in the very center of my being I may have your own perfection dwelling in me. Help me accept and keep your words, and master their divine contents which reveal your will. Then help me to will all that you will.

O my God, let me live day by day in such fellowship with you that I may indeed in everything hear your voice, the living voice of the living God, speaking to me. Let the Holy Spirit, the Spirit of your holiness, be to me your voice guiding me in the path of simple, childlike obedience. I do bless you that I have seen that Christ, in whom I am holy, was the obedient one, that in obedience He sanctified himself to become my sanctification, and that abiding in Him, your obedient, holy Child, is abiding in your will as once done by Him and now to be done by me. O my God, I will indeed obey your will: make me one of your holy nation, a peculiar treasure above all people. Amen.

Personal Application

1. "He became obedient unto death." Though he were a Son, yet learned he obedience by the things which he suffered." "I come to do thy will." "In which will we are sanctified." Christ's example teaches us that obedience is the only path to the holiness or the glory of God. Be this your consecration: a surrender in everything to seek and do the will of God.

2. We are "holy in Christ"—in this Christ who did the will of God and was obedient to the death. We are in Him; in Him we are holy. His obedience is the soil in which we are planted and must be rooted. "It is my meat to do his will"; obedience was the sustenance of His life; in doing God's will He drew down divine nourishment; it must be so with us too.

3. As you study what it is to be and abide in Christ, as you rejoice that you are in Him, always remember it is that same Christ who obeyed in whom God has planted you.

4. If ever you feel perplexed about holiness, just yield yourself again to do God's will, and go and do it. It is ours to obey, it is God's to sanctify.

5. Holy in Christ. Christ sanctified himself by obedience, by doing the will of God, and in that will, as done by Him, we have been sanctified. In accepting that will as done by Him and in accepting Him, I am holy. In accepting that will

of God, as to be done by me, I become holy. I am in Him; in every act of living obedience, I enter into living fellowship with Him, and draw the power of His life into mine.

6. Obedience depends upon hearing the voice. Do not imagine you know the will of God. Pray and wait for the inward teaching of the Spirit.

CHAPTER EIGHT

Holiness and Indwelling

"And let them make me a sanctuary [holy place], that I may dwell among them" (Ex. 25:8).
"And the tent shall be sanctified by my glory . . . and I will dwell among the children of Israel, and will be their God" (Ex. 29:43, 45).

The presence of God makes holy, even when it descends for only a little while, as at Horeb in the burning bush. How much more must that presence make holy the place where it dwells, where it fixes its permanent abode! A vivid example is that the place where God dwells came to be called the holy place, "the holy place of the habitation of the Most High." All around where God dwelt was holy: the holy city, the mountain of God's holiness, His holy house, until we come within the veil to the most holy place—the holy of holies. It is as the indwelling God that He sanctifies His house, that He reveals himself as the Holy One in Israel, that He makes us holy too.

Because God is holy, the house in which He dwells is holy too. Holiness is the only attribute of God which He can communicate to His house, but that He can and does communicate. Among men there is a very close link between the character of a house and its occupants. When there is no obstacle to prevent it, the house unintentionally reflects the master's likeness. Holiness expresses not so much an attribute as the essential being of God in His infinite perfection, and His house testifies to this one truth: He is holy, where He dwells

He must have holiness, and His indwelling makes holy. In His first command to His people to build Him a holy place, God distinctly said that it was that He might dwell among them; the dwelling in the house was to be the shadow of His dwelling in the midst of His people. The house with its holiness thus leads us on to the holiness of His dwelling among His redeemed ones.

The holy place, the habitation of God's holiness, was the center of all God's work in making Israel holy. Everything connected with it was holy. The altar, the priests, the sacrifices, the oil, the bread, the vessels, all were holy because they belonged to God. From the house there issued the two-fold voice—God's call to be holy, God's promise to make holy. God's claim was manifested in the demand for cleansing, for atonement, for holiness, in all who were to draw near, whether as priests or worshipers. And God's promise shone forth from His house in the provision for making holy, in the sanctifying power of the altar, of the blood and the oil. The house embodied the two sides that are united in holiness, the repelling and the attracting, the condemning and the saving. First by keeping the people at a distance, then by inviting and bringing them near, God's house was the great symbol of His own holiness. He had come nigh even to dwell among them; but even so they were not permitted to come near or ever enter the secret place of His presence.

All these things are written on our behalf. As the Indwelling One God is the sanctifier of His people still: the indwelling presence alone makes us holy. This becomes especially clear if we note that the nearer the presence was, the greater the degree of holiness. Because God dwelt among them, the camp was holy: all uncleanness was to be removed from it. But the holiness of the court of the tabernacle was even greater: uncleanness which might not be excluded from the camp would not be tolerated there. The holy place was still holier, because still closer to God. And the inner sanctuary—where the presence dwelt on the mercy seat—was the holiest of all, was most holy. The principle still holds good. Holiness is measured by nearness to God; the more of His presence, the more of true holiness. Perfect indwelling will be perfect holiness. None is holy but the Lord; there is no holiness except in Him. He cannot part with some of His holiness, and give it to us apart from himself; we have only as much of holiness as we have of God himself. And to have Him truly and fully, we must have Him as the Indwelling One. But even His indwelling in a house or place without life or spirit is only a faint shadow of the true indwelling as the Living One, when He enters into and penetrates our very being, and fills us, our very selves, with His own life.

No union is so intimate, so real, so perfect, as that of an indwelling life. Think of the life that circulates through a large and fruitful tree. How it penetrates and fills every portion; how inseparably it unites the whole as long as it exists—in wood and leaf, in flower and fruit, everywhere the indwelling life flows and fills. This life is the life of nature, the life of the Spirit of God which dwells in nature. The same life animates our bodies, the spirit of nature pervading every portion of them with the power of sensibility and action.

Not less intimate, but far more wonderful and real, is the indwelling of the Spirit of the new life, through whom God dwells in the heart of the believer. It is as this indwelling becomes a matter of conscious longing and faith that the soul obeys the command, "Let them make me a holy place, that I may dwell among them," and experiences the truth of the promise, "The tent shall be sanctified by my glory, and I will dwell among the children of Israel."

As the Indwelling One God revealed himself in the Son, whom He sanctified and sent into the world. More than once our Lord insisted, "Believe me, that I am in the Father and the Father in me; the Father abiding in me doeth the works." It is especially as the temple of God that believers are more than once called holy in the New Testament. "The temple of God is holy, which temple ye are." "Your body is a temple of the Holy Spirit." "All the building groweth unto an holy temple in the Lord." It is just because it is through the Spirit that the heart is prepared for the indwelling, and the indwelling effected and maintained that the Spirit so peculiarly takes the attribute of holiness. The indwelling Spirit is the Holy Spirit. The measure of His indwelling, or rather of His revelation of the indwelling Christ, is the measure of holiness.

We have seen what the various degrees of nearness to God's presence in Israel were. They are still to be found.

Some Christians dwell in the camp, but know little of drawing close to the Holy One. Outer-court Christians long for pardon and peace. They always come to the altar of atonement, but know little of true nearness or holiness, or of their privilege as priests to enter the holy place. There are still others who have learned that this is their calling and long to draw near, but even so they hardly understand the boldness they have to enter into the holiest of all and dwell there. They are blessed to whom this secret of the Lord has been revealed. They know what the rent veil means, and the access into the immediate presence. The veil has been taken away from their hearts. They have found the secret of true holiness in the indwelling of the Holy One, the God who is holy and who makes holy.

The God who calls you to holiness is the God of the indwelling life. The tabernacle typifies it, the Son reveals it, the Spirit communicates it and the eternal glory will fully manifest it. And, believer, you may experience it. It is your calling as a believer to be God's holy temple. Only yield yourself to His full indwelling. Do not seek first for holiness in what you are or do; seek it in God. Do not even seek it as a gift from God; seek it in God himself, in His indwelling presence. Worship Him in the beauty of holiness, as He dwells in the high and holy place. And as you worship, listen to His voice: "Thus saith the high and lofty One, that inhabiteth eternity, whose name is Holy: I dwell in the high and holy place, with him also that is of a contrite and humble spirit." As the Spirit strengthens us mightily in the inward man so that Christ dwells in our heart by faith, and as the Father comes and together with Him makes His abode in us—it is then that we are truly holy. In true, wholehearted consecration, let us yield ourselves completely to be the dwelling of the Most High, the habitation of His holiness just as distinctly as were the tabernacle and the temple. A house filled with the glory of God, a heart filled with all the fullness of God, is God's promise; that is our portion. In faith claim and accept and hold fast the blessing; Christ, the Holy One of God, in His Father's name, will enter and take possession. Then faith will bring the solution of all our difficulties, the victory over all our failures, the fulfillment of all our desires. "The tent, the heart, shall be sanctified by my glory; and I will dwell among them." The open secret of true holiness, the secret of the joy unspeakable, is Christ dwelling in the heart by faith.

Prayer

We bow our knees to the Father of our Lord Jesus that He would grant unto us, according to the riches of His glory, what He himself has taught us to ask for. We ask that Christ may dwell in our hearts by faith. We long for that most blessed, permanent, conscious indwelling of the Lord Jesus in the heart, which He so distinctly promised as the fruit of the Holy Spirit's coming. Father, we ask for what Christ meant when He spake of the loving, obedient disciple: "I will come and manifest myself to him. We will come and take up our abode with him." Grant unto us this indwelling of Christ in the heart by faith!

For this, we beseech you to strengthen us with might by your Spirit in the inner man. Most Mighty God, let the spirit of your divine power work mightily within us, renewing our mind, will and affections, so that the heart be thoroughly prepared and furnished as a temple, as a home, for Jesus. Let that blessed Spirit strengthen us to have the faith that receives the blessed Savior and His indwelling presence.

O most Gracious Father, hear our cry. We bow our knee to you. We plead the riches of your glory. We praise you who are mighty to do above all that we can ask or think. We wait on you, our Father, to grant us a mighty strengthening by the Spirit in the inner man that this bliss may be ours in its full blessedness, our Lord Jesus dwelling in the heart.

We ask it in His name. Amen.

Personal Application

1. God's dwelling in the midst of Israel was the great central fact to which all the commands concerning holiness were only preparatory and subordinate. So the work of the Holy Spirit also culminates in the personal indwelling of Christ (John 14:21, 23; Eph. 3:16, 17). Aim at this and expect it.

2. The tabernacle with its three divisions was, as pic-

tured in other spiritual truths, the image of man's threefold nature. Our spirit is the holiest of all, where God is meant to dwell, where the Holy Spirit is given. The life of the soul, with its powers of feeling, knowing, and willing, is the holy place. And the outer life of the body, of conduct and action, is the outer court. Begin by believing that the Spirit dwells in the inmost sanctuary, where His workings are secret and hidden. Honor Him by trusting Him to work, by yielding to Him in silent worship before God. From within He will take possession of thought and will; He will even fill the outer court, the body, with the holiness of God. "The God of peace himself sanctify you wholly; and may your spirit, and soul, and body, be preserved entire, without blame. Faithful is he which calleth you, who will also do it."

3. God's indwelling was within the veil, in the unseen, the secret place. Faith knew it, and served Him with holy fear. Our faith knows that God the Holy Spirit has His abode in the hidden place of our inner life. Set open your inmost being to Him; bow in lowly reverence before the Holy One as you yield yourself to His working. Holiness is the presence of the Indwelling One.

CHAPTER NINE

Holiness and Mediation

"And thou shalt make a plate of pure gold, and grave upon it . . . Holiness to the Lord. . . . And it shall be upon Aaron's forehead, that Aaron may bear the iniquity of the holy things, which the children of Israel shall hallow in all their holy gifts; and it shall be always upon his forehead, that they may be accepted before the Lord" (Ex. 28:36, 38).

God's house was to be the dwelling place of His holiness, the place where He was to reveal himself as the Holy One, not to be approached except with fear and trembling; as the holy-making One, drawing to himself all who would be made partakers of His holiness. The center of the revelation of His holy and holy-making presence is found in the person of the high priest, in his double capacity of representing God with man, and man with God. He is the embodiment of the divine holiness in human form, and of human holiness as a divine gift, as far as the dispensation of symbol and shadow could offer and express it. In him God came near to sanctify and bless the people. In him the people came their very nearest to God. And yet the very Day of Atonement, in which he might enter into the most holy, was only proof of how unholy man was and how unfit to abide in God's presence. In himself a proof of Israel's unholiness, he still was a type and picture of the coming Savior, our blessed Lord Jesus, and a wondrous exhibition of the way in which hereafter the holiness of God should become the portion of His people.

Among the many points in which the high priest typified Christ as our sanctification, perhaps none is more suggestive or beautiful than the holy crown he wore on his forehead. Everything about him was to be holy. His garments were holy garments. But in one thing this holiness reached its fullest manifestation. On his forehead he was always to wear a plate of gold engraved with the words, *Holiness to the Lord*. There everyone read that the whole object of his existence, the one thing for which he lived, was to embody and bear the divine holiness, to be the chosen one through whom God's holiness might flow out in blessing upon the people.

The way in which the blessing of the holy crown was to act was a most remarkable one. In bearing *Holiness to the Lord* on his forehead, he is, we read, "to bear the iniquity of the holy things which the children of Israel shall hallow . . . that they may be accepted before the Lord." For every sin some sacrifice or way of atonement had been devised.

But how about the sin that cleaves to the very sacrifice and religious service itself? "Thou desirest truth in the inward parts." How painfully the worshiper might be oppressed by the consciousness that his penitence, his faith, his love, his obedience, his very consecration, were all imperfect and defiled! Even for this need of the worshiper, God had provided. The holiness of the high priest covered the sin and the unholiness of his holy things. The holy crown was God's pledge that the holiness of the high priest rendered the worshiper acceptable. If he was unholy, there was one who was holy, who had a holiness that could avail for him too, a holiness in which he could trust. He could look to the high priest not only to effect atonement by his blood sprinkling, but also to secure a holiness in his person that made him and his gifts most acceptable. Conscious of personal unholiness, the worshiper might rejoice in a mediator, in the holiness of another than himself, the priest whom God had provided.

Have we not here a most precious lesson, leading us a step farther on in the way of holiness? How does God produce holiness? The divine answer: Through a man whom the Divine Holiness has chosen to rest upon, and whose holiness belongs to us as His brethren, the very members of His own body. Through a holiness which is of such efficacy that the insufficiency of our best intentions is cleansed, and we can enter the holy presence with the assurance of being altogether well-pleasing.

Is not this precisely the lesson that many earnest seekers after holiness need? They know all that the Word teaches of the blessed atonement and the full pardon it has brought. They believe in the Father's wonderful love and what He is ready to do for them. But when they hear of the childlike simplicity and assurance of faith, the loving obedience and blessed surrender with which the Father expects them to come and receive the blessing, their hearts fail for fear—as if the blessing were beyond their reach. What does it help that the Holy One is said to come so close when their unholiness renders them incapable of claiming or grasping the presence that offers itself to them? See how the Holy One here reveals His way of producing holiness and preparing one for the fellowship of His holiness. In His elect One as mediator, holiness is prepared and stored up—enough for all who come through Him. As I pray or worship, and realize how much I lack that humility, fervency and faith that God has a right to demand, I may look up to the High Priest in His holiness, to the holy crown upon His forehead. The words there help me to believe that the iniquity of my best intentions is borne and taken away. With all my deficiency and unworthiness, I may know most assuredly that my prayer is acceptable, a sweet-smelling savour. I may look up to the Holy One to see Him smiling on me for the sake of His anointed one. "The holy crown shall always be on His forehead, that they may be accepted before the Lord." It is the blessed truth of substitution—One for all—of mediatorship, God's way of making us holy. The sacrifice of the worshiping Israelite is holy and acceptable in virtue of the holiness of Another.

The Old Testament shadow can never adequately set forth the New Testament reality with its fullness of grace and truth. As we proceed in our study, we shall find that the holiness of Jesus our sanctification is not only imputed but imparted, because we are in Him; the new man we have put on is created in true holiness. We are not only counted holy, we are holy. We have received a new holy nature in Christ Jesus. "He that sanctifieth and they who are sanctified are all of one; therefore he is not ashamed to call them brethren." Our living union with Jesus, God's holy one, has given us the new and holy nature, and with that a claim and a share in all the holiness there is in Jesus. So, as often as we are conscious of how unholy we are, we have only to come under the covering of the holiness of Jesus to enjoy the full assurance that we and our gifts are most acceptable. No matter how great the weakness of our faith, the shortcoming in our desire for God's glory, or the lack in our love or zeal, when we see Jesus—with holiness to the Lord on His forehead— we lift up our faces to receive the divine smile of full approval and perfect acceptance.

This is God's way of making holy. Not only with the holy place, as we have seen, but with the holy persons too, He begins with a center, and from that in an ever-widening circle makes holy. And that this divine method will be crowned with success we may be sure.

In the Word we find a most remarkable illustration of the extent to which it will be realized. We find the words on the holy crown once again in the Old Testament at its close. In the day of the Lord, "there shall be upon the bells of the horses, *Holiness to the Lord.*" The high priest's motto shall then have become the watchword of daily life—every article of beauty or of service shall be holy too; from the head it shall have extended to the skirts of the garments.

Let us begin with realizing the holiness of Jesus in its power to cover the shortcomings of our walk. Let us put it to the test and no longer allow our unworthiness to keep us back or make us doubt. Believe that our being and our sanctified choices are acceptable because in Christ they are holy to the Lord. Let us live in this consciousness of acceptance and enter into fellowship with the Holy One. As we enter in and abide in the holiness of Jesus, it will enter in and abide in us. It will take possession and spread its conquering power through our whole life, until upon everything that belongs to us the words shall also shine, *Holiness to the Lord.* Again we shall find how God's way of holiness always starts from a center, here the center of our renewed nature, and then spreads throughout the whole circumference of our being to make His holiness prove its power. Let us but dwell under the covering of the holiness of Jesus as He fills up the lack in our daily walk and He will make us and our life holy to the Lord.

Prayer

My God and Father, my soul blesses you for this wonderful revelation of what your way and your grace are with those whom you have called "holy in Christ." You know, Lord, how we have limited the effects of your free acceptance of us by our own attainments and the conscious shortcoming this has wrought. We did not know that in the holiness of Him who makes us holy, there is a divinely infinite efficacy to cover our iniquities and give us the assurance of perfect acceptance. Blessed Father, open our eyes to see and our hearts to understand this holy crown of our blessed Jesus, with its wondrous and blessed, Holiness to the Lord.

When our hearts condemn us, because we do not consciously pray according to the will or for the glory of God, or truly in the name of Jesus, then most Holy Father, be pleased by your Spirit to show us how bright the smile and how hearty the welcome is we still have with you. Teach us to come in the holiness of our High Priest and enter into your holiness until it takes possession of us and permeates our whole being, and all that is in us becomes holy to the Lord. Amen.

Personal Application

1. Holiness is not something I can see or admire in myself: it is covering myself, losing myself, in the holiness of Jesus. How wonderfully this is typified in Aaron and the holy crown. And the more I see and have apprehended of the holiness of Jesus, the less shall I see or seek holiness in myself.

2. He will make me holy. My tempers and dispositions will be renewed. My heart and mind cleansed and sanctified. Holiness will be a new nature. All along there will be the consciousness, humbling and yet joyful—it is not I, Christ lives in me.

3. Bow humbly with an open heart before God that the Holy Spirit may reveal to us what it is to be holy in the

holiness of Another, in the holiness of Jesus, that is, in the holiness of God.

4. Do not struggle too much to grasp this with the intellect. Just believe it and look in simplicity and trust to Jesus to make it all right for you.

5. Holy in Christ. In childlike faith I take Christ's holiness afresh as my covering before God. In loving obedience I take it into my will and life. I trust and I follow Jesus: this is the path of holiness.

6. In our lessons in the Word from Paradise downward, we see that the elements of holiness in us are these, each corresponding to some special aspect of God's holiness: deep restfulness (ch. 3), humble reverence (ch. 4), entire surrender (ch. 5), joyful adoration (ch. 6) simple obedience (ch. 7). These all prepare for the divine Indwelling (ch. 8), and this again we have through the abiding in Jesus with the crown of holiness on His head.

CHAPTER TEN

Holiness and Separation

"I am the Lord your God, which have separated you from other people. And ye shall be holy unto me: for I the Lord am holy, and have severed you from other people, that ye should be mine" (Lev. 20:24, 26).

"Until the days be fulfilled, in the which he separateth himself unto the Lord, he shall be holy. . . . All the days of his separation he is holy unto the Lord" (Num. 6:5, 8).

"Wherefore Jesus also, that he might sanctify the people through his own blood, suffered without the gate. Let us go forth therefore unto him without the camp, bearing his reproach" (Heb. 13:12, 13).

Separation is not holiness, but is the way to it. Though there can be no holiness without separation, there can be separation that does not lead to holiness. It is of deep importance to understand both the difference and the connection that we may be kept from the right-hand error of counting separation alone as holiness, as well as the left-hand error of seeking holiness without separation.

The Hebrew word for holiness possibly comes from a root that means to separate. But where we have in our translation "separate" or "sever" or "set apart," we have quite different words. The word for holy is used exclusively to express that specific idea. Although the idea of holy always includes that of separation, it is itself something infinitely higher. It is of great importance to understand this well, because the being set apart to God, the surrender to His claim, the devotion or consecration to His service, are often spoken of as if these constituted holiness. We cannot too strongly emphasize that these are only the beginning, the presupposition— holiness itself is infinitely more. Not what I am or do or give is holiness, but what God is and gives and does to me. God taking possession of me makes me holy; it is the presence and the glory of God that really makes holy.

A careful study of God's words to Israel will make this clear to us. Eight times we find the expression in Leviticus, "Ye shall be holy, for I am holy." Holiness is the highest attribute of God, expressive not only of His relation to Israel, but of His very being and nature, His infinite moral perfection. Only by very slow and gradual steps can He teach the carnal, darkened mind of man what this means, yet from the very beginning He tells His people that His purpose is that they should be like himself—holy—because and as He is holy. To tell me that God separates men for himself to be His— even as He gives himself to be theirs—tells me of a relationship that exists, but tells me nothing of the real nature of this holy being or of the essential worth of the holiness He will communicate to me. Separation is only the setting apart and taking possession of the vessel to be cleansed and used; it is the filling of it with the precious contents we entrust to it that gives it its real value. Holiness is the divine filling without which the separation leaves us empty. Separation is not holiness.

But separation is essential to holiness. "I have separated you from other people, and ye shall be holy." Until I have chosen and separated a vessel from those around it, and cleansed it, if need be, I cannot fill or use it. I must have it in my hand with full and exclusive command of it for the time being, or I will not pour into it the precious milk or wine. In that way God separated His people when He brought them up out of Egypt, separated them unto himself when He gave them His covenant and His law, that He might have them under His control and power to work out His purpose of making them holy. This He could not do until He had them apart and had awakened in them the consciousness that they were His peculiar people, wholly and only His, until He had so taught them also to separate themselves to Him. Separation is essential to holiness.

The institution of the Nazarite will confirm this, and will also bring out very clearly what separation means. Israel was meant to be a holy nation. Its holiness was especially typified in its priests. With regard to the individual Israelite, we nowhere read in the books of Moses of his being holy. But there were ordinances through which the Israelite, who wanted to prove his desire to be entirely holy, could do so. He might separate himself from the ordinary life of the nation around him and live the life of a Nazarite, a separated one. In those days of shadow and type, this separation was accepted as holiness. "All the days of his separation he is holy unto the Lord."

The separation especially consisted of three things: *temperance*, in abstinence from the fruit of the vine; *humiliation*, in not cutting or shaving his hair ("it is a shame for a man if he have long hair"); *self-sacrifice*, in not defiling himself for even father or mother on their death. What we must particularly note is that the separation was not from things unlawful, but things lawful. There was nothing sinful in itself in Abraham living in his father's house or in Israel dwelling in Egypt. The spirit of separation is manifested in giving up not only what can be proved to be sin, but all that may hinder the full intensity of our surrender into God's hands to make us holy.

What lessons does this truth suggest? We must know the need for separation. It is no arbitrary demand of God, but has its ground in the very nature of things. To separate a thing is to set it free for one special use or purpose, that it may with undivided power fulfill the will of the one who chose it and so realize its destiny. It is the principle that lies at the root of all division of labor; complete separation to one branch of study or labor is the way to success and perfection. Before me is an oak forest with the trees all shooting up straight and close to each other. On the outskirts one tree is separated from the others and its heavy trunk and wide-spreading branches prove that being separated and having a large piece of ground separated for its own use, where roots and branches can spread is the secret of growth and greatness. Our human powers are limited; if God is to take full possession and if we are to enjoy Him fully, separation to Him is nothing but the simple, natural, indispensable requisite. God wants us all to himself that He may give himself completely to us.

We must know the purpose of separation. It is to be found in what God has said, "Ye shall be holy unto me, for I the Lord am holy, and have separated you from the people, that ye should be *mine*." In the deepest sense of the word, God has separated us for himself, that He might enter into us and show forth himself in us. His holiness is the sum and the center of all His perfections. It is that He may make us holy like himself that He has separated us. Separation never has any value in itself; it may become most wrong or hurtful—everything depends upon the purpose in mind for it. It is as God gets and takes full possession of us, as the eternal life in Christ has the mastery of our whole being and the Holy Spirit flows fully and freely through us so that we dwell in God and God in us, that separation will be, not a thing of ordinances and observances, but a spiritual reality. As we see, accept and follow after this purpose of God, difficult questions as to what we must be separated from and how much sacrifice separation demands will find an easy answer. God separates from all that does not lead us into His holiness and fellowship.

Above all, we need to know the power of separation, the power that leads us into it in the spirit of desire and joy, liberty and love. The great separating word in human language is the word mine. In this we have the great source of effort and of happiness: in the child with its toys, in labor with its gains and rewards, in the patriot who dies for his country. This mine lays its hand on that which it sets apart from all else. It is the great word that love uses, whether by the child that says to its mother, "My own mama," that calls forth the response, "My own child"; or the bridegroom who takes the daughter from her beloved home and parents to become his; or whether by the holy God who speaks: "I have separated you from the people, that ye should be mine." Always it is with that mine that love exerts its mighty magnetic power and draws from all else to itself. God himself knows no mightier argument and can put forth no more powerful attraction than this, "that ye should be mine." The power of separation will come to us and work in us just as fully as we yield ourselves to study and realize that holy purpose, to listen for and appropriate that wondrous mine, to be apprehended and possessed by that almighty love.

Divine love does its separating work step by step along a wondrous path. In redemption it prepares the way. Israel is separated from Egypt by the blood of the Lamb and the guiding pillar of fire. In the command, "Come out and be separate," it awakens man to action. In the promise, "I will be your God," it stirs desire and strengthens faith. In all the holy saints and servants of God—and at last in Him who was holy, harmless, undefiled and separate from sinners—it points the way. In the power of the Holy Spirit, the Spirit of holiness, it seals the separation by the presence of the indwelling God. This is indeed the power of separation. The separating power of the presence of God—it is this we need to know.

"Wherein now shall it be known that I have found grace in thy sight, I and thy people?" said Moses. "Is it not in that thou goest with us? so shall we be separated, I and thy people, from all the people that are upon the face of the earth." The consciousness of God's indwelling presence, making and keeping us His very own, works true separation from the world and its spirit, from ourselves and our own will. As we accept this separation and prize and persevere in it, the holiness of God will enter and take possession. Then we shall realize that to be the Lord's property, a people of His own, signifies infinitely more than merely to be accounted or acknowledged as His—it means that God, in the power and indwelling of the Holy Ghost, fills our being, our affections, and our will with His own life and holiness. He separates us for himself, and sanctifies us to be His dwelling. He comes himself to take personal possession by the indwelling of Christ in the heart. Then we are truly separate, and kept separate, by the presence of God within us.

Prayer

O my God, who has separated me for yourself, I beseech you by your mighty power to make this divine separation deed and truth to me. Within the depths of my own spirit, and without, in all my relationships, the crown of separation of my God be upon me.

I pray especially for you to perfect in power the separation

*from self! Let your presence in the indwelling of my Lord
Jesus be the power that banishes self from the throne. I have
turned from it with abhorrence. Father, reveal your Son fully
in me! It is His enthronement in my heart that can keep me
as your own, as He takes the place of myself.*

*In my outward life, Lord, give me grace to wait for divine
wisdom, to know how to witness for your glory and to meet
the need of your people. Give me grace for the blessedness of
a complete surrender of everything for God, a separation that
holds back nothing, to be His and His alone.*

*Holy Lord God, visit your people. Withdraw them from the
world and from conformity to it. Separate, Lord, separate your
own for yourself. Separate the wheat from the chaff, separate
as by fire the gold from the dross so that it may be seen who
are the Lord's, who are His holy ones. Amen.*

Personal Application

1. Love separates effectually. With what jealousy a hus-
band claims his wife, a mother her children, a miser his
possessions! Pray that the Holy Spirit may show how God
brought you to himself that you should be His. He is a holy
God; He is a jealous God. God's love shed abroad in the heart
makes separation easy.

2. Death separates effectually. If I reckon myself to be
indeed dead in Christ, I am separated from self by the power
of Christ's death. Life separates still more mightily. As I say,
"Not I, but Christ liveth in me," I am lifted up out of the life
of self.

3. Separation must be manifest. It is meant as a witness
to others and ourselves. It must find expression in the external if internally it is to be real and strong. It is the characteristic of a symbolic action that it not merely expresses a
feeling, but nourishes and strengthens the feeling to which
it corresponds. When the soul enters the fellowship of God,
it feels the need of external separation, sometimes even from
what appears to others harmless. If animated by the spirit
of lowly consecration to God, the external may be a great
strengthening of the true separateness.

4. Separation to God and appropriation by Him go together. This has been the blessing that has come to martyrs,

confessors, missionaries—all who have forsaken all.

5. Separation begins in love and ends in love. The spirit of separation is the spirit of self-sacrifice, of surrender to the love of God. The truly separate one will be the most loving and love-winning, yielded to serve God and man. Is not what separates, what distinguishes Jesus from all others, His self-sacrificing love? This is His separateness in which we are to be made like Him.

6. God's holiness is His separateness. Let us enter into His separateness from the world; that will be our holiness. Unite yourself to God. Then you will be separate and holy. God separates for himself, not by an act from without, but as His will and presence take possession of us.

CHAPTER ELEVEN

The Holy One of Israel

"For I am the Lord that bringeth you up out of the land of Egypt, to be your God: ye shall therefore be holy, for I am holy. . . . I the Lord, which sanctify you, am holy" (Lev. 11:45; 21:8).

"I am the Lord thy God, the Holy One of Israel, thy Saviour. . . . Thus saith the Lord, your redeemer, the Holy One of Israel . . . I am the Lord, your Holy One, the creator of Israel, your King" (Isa. 43:3, 14, 15).

Exodus shows God making provision for the holiness of His people. In the holy times and holy places, holy persons, holy things, and holy services, He had taught His people that everything around Him, that all that would come near Him, must be holy. He would dwell only in the midst of holiness. His people must be a holy people. But there is no direct mention of God himself as holy. In the book of Leviticus we are led a step further. Here for the first time God speaks of His own holiness, and makes it the plea for the holiness of His people, as well as its pledge and power. Without this the revelation of holiness would be incomplete and the call to holiness powerless. True holiness will come to us as we learn that God alone is holy. He alone makes holy. Only as we come to Him and in obedience and love are linked to Him can His holiness rest on us.

From the books of Moses onward we shall find that the name of God as holy is seldom found in the inspired writings until we come to Isaiah, the evangelist prophet. There it occurs twenty-six times, and has its true meaning revealed in the way in which it is linked with the name of Savior and Redeemer. The senti-

77

ments of joy and trust and praise with which a redeemed people would look upon their Deliverer are all mentioned in connection with the name of the Holy One.*

"Cry aloud and shout, thou inhabitant of Zion, for great is the Holy One of Israel in the midst of thee." "The poor among men shall rejoice in the Holy One of Israel." "Thou shalt rejoice in the Lord, and shalt glory in the Holy One of Israel."

In Paradise we saw that God the Creator was God the Sanctifier, perfecting the work of His hands. In Israel we saw that God the Redeemer was ever God the Sanctifier, making holy the people He had chosen for himself. Here in Isaiah we see how God the Sanctifier, the Holy One, is to bring about the great redemption of the New Testament: as the Holy One, He is the Redeemer. God redeems because He is holy and loves to make holy: holiness will be redemption perfected. Redemption and holiness together are to be found in the personal relationship to God. The key to the secret of holiness is offered to each believer in that word: "Thus saith the Lord, your redeemer, the Holy One of Israel: I am the Lord, your Holy One." To come near, to know, to possess the Holy One, and be possessed of Him, is holiness.

If God's holiness is thus the only hope for ours, it is right that we seek to know what that holiness is. Although we may find it indeed to be something that is beyond our understanding, it will be helpful to see what has been revealed in the Word concerning it. Let us do so in the spirit of holy fear and worship, trusting the Holy Spirit to be our teacher.

---

*"For I am the Lord your God: ye shall therefore sanctify [make holy] yourselves, and be holy, for I am holy" (Lev. 11:44).

"For I am the Lord that bringeth you up out of the land of Egypt to be your God: ye shall therefore be holy, for I am holy" (Lev. 11:45).

"Ye shall be holy: for I the Lord your God am holy" (Lev. 19:2).

"Sanctify [make holy] yourselves therefore, and be ye holy: for I am the Lord your God. And ye shall keep my statutes and do them: I am the Lord which sanctify you" (Lev. 20:7, 8).

"And ye shall be holy unto me: for I the Lord am holy, and have separated you from other people, that ye should be mine" (Lev. 20:26).

"[The priest] . . . shall be holy unto thee, for I the Lord which sanctify you, am holy" (Lev. 21:8).

"I will be hallowed among the children of Israel: I am the Lord which hallow you" (Lev. 22:32).

"I the Lord do sanctify them" (Lev. 21:23; 22:9, 16).

First notice how this holiness of God—though often mentioned as one of the divine attributes—can hardly be considered as on the same level with the others. The other attributes all refer to some special aspect or characteristic of the divine nature; holiness appears to express the very essence or perfection of the divine being himself. None of the attributes can be predicated of all that belongs to God; but Scripture speaks of His holy name, His holy day, His holy habitation, His holy Word. In the word *holy* we have the nearest possible approach to a summary of all the divine perfections, the description of what Divinity is. We speak of the other attributes as divine perfections, but in this we have the only human expression for the Divine Perfection itself. For this reason theologians have found much difficulty in framing a definition that can express all the word means.

The original Hebrew word (whether derived from a root signifying to separate or another with the idea of shining) expressed the idea of something distinguished from others, separate from them by superior excellence. God is separate and different from all that is created. He keeps himself separate from all that is not God. As the Holy One He maintains His divine glory and perfection against whatever might interfere with it. "There is none holy, but the Lord"; "To whom will you liken me? or shall I be equal? saith the Holy One." In referring to His holiness, God is indeed the Incomparable One; holiness is His alone; there is nothing like it in heaven or earth, except when He gives it. So our holiness will consist, not in a human separation in which we attempt to imitate God's, but rather in entering into His separateness, belonging entirely to Him, set apart by Him for himself.

Closely connected with this is the idea of exaltation: "Thus saith the high and holy One, whose name is Holy." It was the Holy One who was seen sitting upon a throne high and lifted up, the object of the worship of the seraphim. In Psalm 99 God's holiness is especially connected with His exaltation. For this reason, too, His holiness is often linked with His glory and majesty (see "Sixth Day"). Here our holiness will be revealed as the poverty and humility which comes when "the loftiness of man is brought low, and the Lord alone is exalted."

If we ask what comprises the infinite excellence of this separateness and exaltation, we think of divine purity, not only in its negative aspect as hatred of sin, but with the more positive element of perfect beauty. Because we are sinners and the revelation of God's holiness is in a world of sin, it is natural and right that the first and abiding impression of God's holiness should be that of an infinite purity that cannot look upon sin, in whose presence the sinner can only hide his face and tremble. The righteousness of God, forbidding and condemning and punishing sin, has its root in His holiness and is one of its two elements—the devouring and destroying power of the consuming fire. "God that is holy shall be sanctified in righteousness" (Isa. 5:16); in righteousness the holiness of the Holy One is maintained and revealed.

But light not only discovers what is impure, that it may be purified, but is in itself a thing of infinite beauty. Some of our holiest men have not hesitated to speak of God's holiness as the infinite pulchritude or beauty of the Divine Being, the perfect purity and beauty of that light in which God dwells. If the holiness of God is to become ours, to rest upon and enter into us, there must be a constant holy fear that trembles to think of grieving the infinite sensitiveness of this Holy One by our sins. Side by side and in perfect harmony with that fear will be the deep longing to behold the beauty of the Lord, an admiration of His divine glory and a joyful surrender to be His alone.

We must go one step further. When God says, "I am holy: I make holy," we see that one of the chief elements of His holiness is this, that it seeks to communicate itself, to make others partake of its own perfection and blessedness. This is love. In the wonderful revelation in Isaiah of what the Holy One is to His people, we must beware of misreading God's precious Word. It does not say that *although* God is the Holy One and hates sin and ought to punish and destroy, that notwithstanding this He will save. By no means. But we are taught that as the Holy One, just because He is the Holy One, who delights to make holy, He will be the deliverer of His people (see Hos. 11:9). It is holiness above all else that we are invited to look to, to trust in, to rejoice in. The Holy One is the holy-making One. He redeems and saves so that He may win our confidence for himself, so that He may draw us to himself as the Holy One, so that in the personal attachment to Him we may learn to obey and become of one mind with Him, to be holy as He is holy.

The divine holiness is thus that infinite perfection of Divinity in which righteousness and love are in perfect harmony, out of which they proceed, and which together they reveal. It is that energy of the divine life in the power of which God not only keeps himself free from all creature weakness or sin, but unceasingly seeks to lift the creature into union with himself and into the full participation of His own purity and perfection. The glory of God as God, as the God of Creation and Redemption, is His holiness. It is in this that the separateness and exaltation of God, even above man's comprehension, really consists. "God is light"; in His infinite purity He reveals all darkness, and yet has no fellowship with it. He judges and condemns it; He saves out of it, and lifts up into the fellowship of His own purity and blessedness. This is the Holy One of Israel.

It is this God who speaks to us, "I am the Lord your God; I am holy; I make holy." It is in the adoring contemplation of His holiness, in the trustful surrender to it, in the loving fellowship with himself, the Holy One, that we can be made holy.

Do you want to be holy? Then let God's words sink into your heart—"your Holy One." Come and claim Him as your God; claim all that He, as the Holy One who makes holy, can do for you. Only remember that holiness is He himself. Come to Him; worship Him; give Him the glory. Even from Him seek not holiness in yourself; let self be abased and be content that the holiness is His. As His presence fills your heart, as His holiness and glory are your delight—as the Holy One becomes all in all to you—you will be holy with the holiness He loves to see. And as, to the end, you see nothing to admire in self and only beauty in Him, you will know that He has laid of His glory on you; and your holiness will be found in the song, "There is none holy, but the Lord."

Prayer

O God, we have again heard the wonderful revelation of yourself, "I am holy." As we saw how infinitely exalted above all our conceptions your holiness is, we heard your call—almost more wonderful—"Be ye holy, as I am holy." But as every thought of how we were to be holy as you are holy dismayed us, we heard your voice once again, in this most wonderful word of all, "I make you holy." I am "your Holy One."

Most Holy God, we beseech you to help us realize how unholy we are, and so to take the place that is fitting in your presence. Reveal the sinfulness of our nature and all that is of self so that it may no longer be possible to live in it! May the light that reveals this also reveal how your holiness is our only hope, our sure refuge, our complete deliverance. O Lord, by your Spirit speak to our souls the words "the Holy One, your Redeemer" and "your Holy One" with such power that our faith may grow into the assured confidence that we can be holy as you are holy.

Holy Lord God, we wait for you; reveal yourself in power within us and fit us to be the messengers of your holiness, to tell your people how holy you are, and how holy we must be, and how holy you will make us. Amen.

Personal Application

1. This Holy One is God Almighty. Before He revealed himself to Israel as the Holy One, He made himself known to Abraham as the Almighty, "who quickeneth the dead." In all your dealings with God for holiness, remember He is the Almighty One who can do wonders in you. Say often, "Glory to Him who is mighty to do exceeding abundantly above all we ask or think."

2. This Holy One is the righteous God, a consuming fire. Cast yourself into it, so that all that is sinful may be destroyed. As you lay yourself upon the altar, expect the fire. "And yield your members unto God as instruments of righteousness."

3. This Holy One is the God of love. He is your Father; yield yourself to let the Holy Spirit cry in you, "Abba, Father!" That is, let Him shed abroad and fill your heart with God's father-love. God's holiness is His fatherliness; our holiness is child-likeness. Be simple, loving, trustful.

4. This Holy One is God. Let Him be God to you: ruling all, filling all, working all. Worship Him, come near to Him, live with and in and for Him: He will be your holiness.

CHAPTER TWELVE

The Thrice Holy One

*"I saw also the Lord sitting upon a throne, high and lifted up. . . .
Above [Him] stood the seraphims. . . . And one cried unto another,
and said, Holy, holy, holy, is the Lord of hosts: the whole earth is
full of his glory"* (Isa. 6:1–3).

*"And the four beasts . . . they have no rest day and night, saying,
Holy, holy, holy, Lord God Almighty, which was, and is, and is to
come"* (Rev. 4:8).

Not only on earth, but in heaven too, is the holiness of
God His chief and most glorious attribute. And not only on
earth, but in heaven too, the highest inspiration of adoration
and praise mentions His holiness. The brightest of living
beings, they who are ever before and around and above the
throne, find their glory in adoring and proclaiming the holiness of God. Surely for us too there can be no higher honor
than to study and know, to worship and adore, to proclaim
and show forth the glory of the Thrice Holy One.

After Moses Isaiah was the chief messenger of the holiness of God. Each of them had a special preparation for his
commission to make known the Holy One. Moses saw the
Holy One in the fire, and hid his face and feared to look upon
God, and so was prepared to be His messenger and to praise
Him as "glorious in holiness." Isaiah heard the song of the
seraphim, saw the fire on the altar and the house filled with
the smoke, and he cried out, "Woe is me!" In the deep sense
of the need of cleansing, he received the touch of the fire and

the purging of his sin. Only then might he bear to Israel the gospel of the Holy One as its redeemer. May it be in the spirit of fear and lowly worship that we listen to the song of the seraphim, and seek to know and worship the Thrice Holy One. May we too be cleansed with fire that we may be found fit to tell God's people that He is the Holy One of Israel, their redeemer.

The threefold repetition of *Holy* by the Church of Christ has at all times been connected with the Holy Trinity. The song of the living creatures around the throne (Rev. 4) is evidence of this. There we find it followed by the adoration of Him who was and is and is to come, the Almighty: the Eternal Source, the present manifestation in the Son, the future perfecting of the revelation of God in the Spirit's work in His Church. The truth of the Holy Trinity is often regarded as an abstract doctrine, with little direct bearing on practical life. So far is this from being the case that a living faith must be rooted in it. Some spiritual insight into the relation and the operation of each of the Three and the reality of their living oneness is an essential element of true growth in knowledge and spiritual understanding.* Let us here regard the Trinity especially in its relation to God's holiness and as the source of ours. What does it mean that we adore the Thrice Holy One? God is not only holy, but makes holy: in the revelation of the three persons we have the revelation of the way in which God makes holy.

The Trinity teaches us that God has revealed himself in two ways. The Son is the form of God, His manifestation as He shows himself to man, the image in which His unseen glory is embodied and to which man is to be conformed. The

---

*The Divine necessity and meaning of the doctrine of the Trinity is seen from the counter part we have of it in nature. In every living object that exists, we distinguish first the life, then the form or shape in which that life manifests itself, then the power or effect as seen in the result which the life acting in its form or manifestation produces. And so we have God as the unseen one, the fountain of life; the Son as the form or image of God, the manifestation of the unseen life; and the Holy Spirit as the power of that life proceeding from the Father and the Son, and working out the purpose of God's will in the Church. Applying this thought to God as the Holy One, we shall understand better the place of the Son and the Spirit as they bring to us the holiness of God.

Spirit is the power of God, working in man and leading him up to that image. In Jesus, He who had been in the form of God took the form of man, and the Divine Holiness was literally manifested in the form of a human life and the members of a human body. A new holy human nature was formed in Christ, to be communicated to us. In His death His own personal holiness was perfected as human obedience, and so the power of sin was conquered and broken. Therefore in the resurrection, through the Spirit of holiness, He was declared to be the Son of God with power to impart His life to us. There the Spirit of holiness was set free from the veil of the flesh, the trammels that hindered it, and obtained power to enter and dwell in man. The Holy Spirit was poured out as the fruit of resurrection and ascension. Now the Spirit is the power of God in us, working upwards toward Christ, to reproduce His life and holiness in us, to fit us for fully receiving and showing forth Him in our lives. Christ from above comes to us as the embodiment of the unseen holiness of God: the Spirit from within lifts us up to meet Him, and fits us to receive and make our own all that is in Him.

The Triune God whom we adore is the Thrice Holy One. The mystery of the Trinity is the mystery of holiness. The glory and the power of the Trinity is the glory and power of God who makes us holy. There is God dwelling in light inaccessible, a consuming fire of holy love, destroying all that resists, glorifying into its own purity all that yields. There is the Son, casting himself into that consuming fire—whether in its eternal blessedness in heaven, or its angry wrath on earth—a willing sacrifice to be its food and its satisfaction, as well as the revelation of its power to destroy and to save. And there is the Spirit of holiness, the flames of that mighty fire spreading on every side, convicting and judging as the Spirit of burning, and then transforming into its own brightness and holiness all that it can reach. All the relations of the three persons to each other and to us have their root and their meaning in the revelation of God as the Holy One. As we know and partake of Him, we shall know and partake of holiness.

How shall we know Him?

Let us learn to know the holiness of God as the seraphs do: in the worship of the Thrice Holy One. With veiled faces let us join in the ceaseless song of adoration: "Holy, holy, holy, is the Lord of hosts." Each time we meditate on the Word, each prayer to the Holy God, each act of faith in Christ the Holy One, each exercise of waiting dependence on the Holy Spirit, let it be in the spirit of worship: Holy, holy, holy.

Let us learn to know the holiness of God as Isaiah did. He was to be the chosen messenger to reveal and interpret to the people the name, the Holy One of Israel. His preparation was the vision that made him cry out, "Woe is me! for mine eyes have seen the King, the Lord of hosts." Let us bow in silence before the Holy One until our comeliness too be turned into corruption. Let us feel the cleansing fire from the altar, the touch of the live coals of the burning holiness, which not only consumes but purges lips and heart to say, "Here am I, send me."

Let us worship, whether like the adoring seraphim, or like the trembling prophet, until we know that our service too is accepted, to tell forth the praise of the Thrice Holy One.

If we are indeed to be the messengers of the Holy One, let us seek to enter fully into what thrice holy means. *Holy, the Father,* God above us, high and lifted up, whom no man hath seen or can see, whose holiness none dare approach, but who himself draws near in His holiness to make holy. *Holy, the Son,* God with us, revealing divine holiness in human life, maintaining it amid the suffering of death for us, and preparing a holy life and nature for His people. *Holy, the Spirit,* God in us, the power of holiness within us, reaching out to and embracing Christ, and transforming our inner life into the union and communion with Him in whom we are holy. This is perfect holiness—the divine Thrice Holy: holiness hidden and unapproachable, holiness manifested in human nature, holiness communicated and made our very own.

The mystery of the Holy Trinity is the mystery of the Christian life, the mystery of holiness. The three are one, and we need to enter ever more deeply into the truth that none of the three ever works separately or independently of the others. The Son reveals the Father, and the Father reveals the Son. The Father gives not himself, but the Spirit: the Spirit speaks not of himself, but cries Abba, Father! The Son is our sanctification, our life, our all: the fullness is in

Him. And yet we must always bow our knees to the Father for Him to reveal Christ in us, for Him to establish us in Christ. The Father does not do this without the Spirit; we have to ask to be strengthened mightily by the Spirit that Christ may dwell in us. Christ gives the Spirit to them that believe and love and obey; the Spirit again gives Christ, formed within and dwelling in the heart. So in each act of worship, each step of growth, each blessed experience of grace, all three persons are actively engaged. The one is ever three, the three are ever one.

To apply this in the life of holiness, faith in the Holy Trinity must be a living practical reality:

In every prayer to the Father to sanctify you, take up your position in Christ, and do it in the power of the Spirit within you.

In every exercise of faith in Christ as your sanctification, let your posture be that of prayer to the Father and trust in Him as He delights to honor the Son, and of quiet expectancy of the Spirit's working, through whom the Father glorifies the Son.

In every surrender of the soul to the sanctification of the Spirit, to His leading as the Spirit of holiness, look to the Father who grants His mighty working and who sanctifies through faith in the Son, and expect the Spirit's power to manifest itself in showing the will of God and Jesus as your sanctification.

If for a time this appears to contradict the simplicity of childlike faith and prayer, be assured that as God has thus revealed himself, He will teach you so to worship and believe. Then holy, holy, holy will become the deep undertone of all our worship and all our life.

Children of God, called to be holy as He is holy, let us bow down and worship in His holy presence! Come and veil the face. Turn away from gazing at that which is beyond our comprehension and let the soul be gathered into that inner stillness in which the worship of the heavenly sanctuary alone can be heard. Come and cover the feet. Withdraw from the busyness of work—be it worldly or religious—and learn to worship. Come and fall down in self-abasement to let the glory of the Holy One shine upon you. And as you hear and join in singing the song, Holy, holy, holy, you will discover that in such knowledge and worship of the Thrice Holy One is the power that makes you holy.

Prayer

Holy, holy, holy, the Lord God Almighty! which was and is and is to come! I worship you as the Triune God. With face veiled and feet covered, I would bow in deep humility and silence, till your mercy lift me as on eagles' wings to behold your glory.

Most merciful God, who hast called me to be holy as you are holy, reveal to me somewhat of your holiness! As it shines upon me and strikes death into the creature and the flesh, may even the most involuntary taint of sin and its slightest movement become unbearable. As it shines and revives the hope of being partaker of your holiness, may the confidence grow strong that you yourself are making me holy and will even make me a messenger of your holiness.

Thrice holy God, I worship you as my God. Holy is the Father; holy and making holy; making holy His Son and sending Him into the world that we might behold the very glory of God in a human face, the face of Jesus Christ. Holy is the Son, the Holy One of God, fulfilling the will of the Father, and so making holy himself that He might be our holiness. Holy is the Spirit, the Spirit of holiness, dwelling within us, making the Son and His holiness our own, and so making us partakers of the holiness of God. O my God, I bow down and worship and adore!

May even now the worship of heaven that rests not day or night be the worship my soul renders to you without ceasing. May its song be, down in the depths of the heart, the keynote of my life: Holy, holy, holy, Lord God Almighty! which was and is and is to come. Amen.

Personal Application

1. Thought always needs to distinguish and separate: in life alone there is perfect unity. The more we know the living God, the more we shall realize how truly the Three are One. In each act of one person the other two are present. There is not a prayer that rises but the presence of the Holy Three is

needed: through Christ, in the Spirit, we speak to the Father.

2. To apprehend this in faith is to have the secret of holiness. The Holy God above us, ever giving and working; the Holy One of God, the living gift, who has possession of us, in whom we are; the Holy Spirit, God within us, through whom the Father works, and the Son is revealed: this is the God who says, "I am holy, I make holy." In the perfect unity of the work of the three, holiness is found.

3. No wonder that the love of the Father and the grace of the Son do not accomplish more, when the fellowship of the Holy Spirit is little understood or sought or accepted. The Holy Spirit is the fruit and crown of the divine revelation, through whom the Son and the Father come to us. If you would know God, if you would be holy, you must be taught and led of the Spirit.

4. Whenever you worship the Thrice Holy One, hearken if no voice be heard: "Whom shall I send, and who will go for us?" Let the answer rise, "Here am I, send me," and offer yourself to be a messenger of the holiness of God to those around you.

5. When in meditation and worship you have tried to take in and express what God's Word has taught, then comes the time for confessing how you know nothing, and for waiting on God to reveal himself.

CHAPTER THIRTEEN

Holiness and Humility

"For thus saith the high and lofty One that inhabiteth eternity, whose name is Holy; I dwell in the high and holy place, with him also that is of a contrite and humble spirit, to revive the spirit of the humble, and to revive the heart of the contrite ones" (Isa. 57:15).

Very wonderful is the revelation we have in Isaiah of God, the Holy One, as the Redeemer and the Savior of His people. In the midst of the people whom He created and formed for himself, He will dwell as the Holy One, showing forth His power and His glory, filling them with joy and gladness. All these promises, however, refer to the people as a whole. Our text today reveals a new and especially beautiful feature of the divine holiness in its relation to the individual. The high and lofty One, whose name is Holy and whose only fit dwelling place is eternity, looks to the man who is of a humble and contrite heart; with him will He dwell. God's holiness is His condescending love. It is a consuming fire against all who exalt themselves before Him, but to the spirit of the humble it is like the shining of the sun, heart-reviving and life-giving.

The deep significance of this promise comes out clearly when we connect it with the other promises of New Testament times. The great feature of the New Covenant, in its superiority to the old, is that whereas in the law and its institution all was external, in the New the kingdom of God would be within. God's laws are given and written into the

90

heart, a new spirit is put within us, God's own Spirit is given to dwell within our spirit, and so the heart and the inner life are fitted to be the temple and home of God. These constitute the peculiar privileges of the ministration of the Spirit. Our text is perhaps the only one in the Old Testament in which this indwelling of the Holy One—not only among the people but in the heart of the individual believer—is clearly brought out. In this the two aspects of the divine holiness would reach their full manifestation: I dwell in the high and holy place, and with him also that is of a contrite and humble spirit. In His heaven above, the high and lofty place, and in our heart, contrite and humble, God has His home. God's holiness is His glory that separates Him by an infinite distance, not only from sin but even from the creature, lifting Him high above it. God's holiness is His love, drawing Him down to the sinner, so that He may lift him into His fellowship and likeness, and make him holy as He is holy. The Holy One seeks the humble; the humble find the Holy One. Such are the two lessons we have to learn.

The Holy One seeks the humble. Nothing has such an attraction for God and such affinity with holiness as a contrite and humble spirit. The reason is evident. There is no law in the natural and the spiritual world more simple than that two bodies cannot at the same moment occupy the same space. Only to the extent that the new occupant can empty the space of what it was filled with before can it really possess. In man, self has possession and self-will the mastery—there is no room for God. It is impossible for God to dwell or rule when self is on the throne. Sin and self-love have a blinding influence, and often the believer is not truly conscious of the extent to which self-will reigns. Until it is revealed by God's Spirit, there can be no true contrition or humility. But then when the soul sees how self has been secretly keeping out God, with what shame it is broken down and how it longs to break utterly away from self that God may have His place! This brokenness, and continued breaking down, is expressed by the word contrition. When the soul sees how foolish and how guilty it has been secretly honoring self and by that keeping the Holy One from the place which He alone has a right to and which He would so blessedly have filled, it casts itself down in utter self-abasement with one desire alone—to be nothing and to give God the place and the praise that is His due.

Such breaking down and humiliation is painful. Its intense reality consists in this, that the soul can see nothing in itself to trust or hope in. And least of all can it imagine that it should be an object of divine complacency or a fit vessel for the divine blessing. But this is just the message which the Word of the Lord brings to our faith. It tells us that the Holy One, who dwells in the high and lofty place, is seeking and preparing for himself a dwelling here on this earth. It tells us something the truly contrite and humble could never imagine and even now can hardly believe, that it is with such people, and only such, that God will dwell. These are they in whom God can be glorified, in whom there is room for Him to take the place of self and to fill the emptied place with himself. The Holy One seeks the humble. Just when we see that there is nothing in us to admire or rest in, God sees in us everything to admire and to rest in, because there is room for himself. The lowly one is the home of the Holy One.

The humble find the Holy One. Just when the consciousness of sin and weakness, and the discovery of how much self there is, makes you fear that you can never be holy, the Holy One gives himself. Not as you look at self, and seek to know whether now you are contrite and humble—no, but when no longer looking at self, because you have given up all hope of seeing anything in it but sin, you look up to the Holy One, you will see how His promise is your only hope. It is in faith that the Holy One is revealed to the contrite soul. Faith is always the opposite of what we see and feel; it looks to God alone. Faith believes—in its deepest consciousness of unholiness, and its fear that it never can be holy—that God, the Holy One who makes holy, is near as Redeemer and Savior. It is content to be low, in the consciousness of unworthiness and emptiness, and still to rejoice in the assurance that God himself does take possession and revive the heart of the contrite one. Happy the soul who is willing to learn soon the lesson that it always is going to be the simultaneous experience of weakness and power; of emptiness and filling; of deep, real humiliation and the real and most wonderful indwelling of the Holy One.

This is indeed the deep mystery of the divine life. To human reason it is a paradox. When Paul says of himself, "as dying, and behold we live; as sorrowful, yet always rejoicing; as having nothing, yet possessing all things," he only gives expression to the law of the kingdom: *as self is displaced and man becomes nothing, God will become all.* Side by side with the deepest sense of nothingness and weakness, the sense of infinite riches and the joy unspeakable can fill the heart. However deep and blessed the experience becomes of the nearness, the blessing, the love, the actual indwelling of the Holy One, it is never an indwelling in the old self; it is ever a divine presence humbling self to make place for God alone to be exalted. The power of Christ's death, the fellowship of His cross, works each moment side by side with the power and the joy of His resurrection. "He that humbleth himself shall be exalted"; in the blessed life of faith the humiliation and the exaltation are simultaneous, each dependent on the other.

The humble find the Holy One; and when they have found Him, the possession only humbles all the more. Not that there is no danger or temptation of the flesh exalting itself in the possession, but knowing the danger, the humble soul seeks for grace to fear continually, with a fear that only clings more firmly to God alone. Never for a moment imagine that you attain a state in which self or the flesh are absolutely dead. No. By faith you enter into and abide in a fellowship with Jesus, in which self and flesh are crucified. Abiding in Him, you are free from their power—but only as you believe and in believing have gone out of self and dwell in Jesus. Therefore, the more abundant God's grace becomes and the more blessed the indwelling of the Holy One, keep all the lower, more humble. Your danger is greater, but your Help is now nearer. Be content in trembling to confess the danger; it will make you bold in faith to claim the victory.

Believers, who profess to be nothing, and to trust in grace alone, I pray you, listen to the wondrous message. The high and lofty One—whose name is Holy, and who dwells in the holy place and who can dwell nowhere but in a holy place—seeks a dwelling here on earth. Will you give it Him? Will you not fall down in the dust that He may find in you the humble heart He loves to dwell in? Will you not now believe that even in you, however low and broken you feel, He delights to make His dwelling? "Blessed are the poor in spirit: for theirs is the kingdom"; with them the King dwells. This is the path to holiness—be humble, and the holy nearness and presence of God in you will be your holiness. As you hear the command, Be holy, as I am holy, by faith claim the promise and answer, I will be holy, O Most Holy God, if you, the Holy One, will dwell with me.

Prayer

O Lord, you are the high and lofty One, whose name is Holy. And still you say, "I dwell in the high and holy place, and with him that is of a contrite and humble spirit." Yes, Lord, when the soul takes the low place, and has low thoughts of itself, when it feels it is nothing, you love to come and comfort, to dwell with it and revive it.

O my God! my creature nothingness humbles me. My many transgressions humble me. My innate sinfulness humbles me. But this humbles me most of all—your infinite condescension and the ineffable indwelling you so graciously offer. It is your holiness, in Christ bearing our sin, your holy love bearing with our sin and consenting to dwell in us; O God, this love that passes knowledge humbles me. I do beseech you, let it do its work until self hides its head and flees away at the presence of your glory, and you alone are all.

Holy Lord God! I pray you to humble me. Did you not long ago meet your servants and show yourself to them until they fell upon their faces and feared? My God, you know I have no humility which I can bring you. In my blessed Savior, who humbled himself in the form of a servant and unto the death of the cross, I hide myself. In Him, in His spirit and likeness, I would live before you. Work in me, by the Holy Spirit dwelling in me, and as I am dead to self in Him and His cross makes me nothing, let your holy indwelling revive and quicken me. Amen.

Personal Application

1. Lowliness and holiness. Hold fast the intimate connection. Lowliness is taking the place that becomes me; ho-

liness is giving God the place that becomes Him. If I be nothing before Him, and God be all to me, I am in the sure path of holiness. Lowliness is holiness, because it gives all the glory to God.

2. "Blessed are the poor in spirit, for theirs is the kingdom of heaven." These first words of the Master when He opened His lips to proclaim the Kingdom, are often the last in the hearts of His disciples. "The Kingdom is in the Holy Ghost"; to the poor in spirit, those who know they have nothing that is really spiritual, the Holy Spirit comes to their life. The poor in spirit are the kingdom of the saints: in them the Holy Spirit reveals the King.

3. Many strive hard to be humble with God, but with men they maintain their rights and nourish self. Remember that the great school of humility before God is to accept the humbling of man. Christ sanctified himself in accepting the humiliation and injustice which evil men laid upon Him.

4. Humility never sees its own beauty, because it refuses to look to itself; it only wonders at the condescension of the Holy God, and rejoices in the humility of Jesus, God's Holy One, our Holy One.

5. The link between holiness is indwelling. The lofty One, whose name is Holy, dwells with the contrite one. And where He dwells is the holy place.

CHAPTER FOURTEEN

The Holy One of God

"Therefore also that holy thing which shall be born of thee shall be called the Son of God" (Luke 1:35).
"We believe and are sure that thou art that Christ, the Son of the living God" (John 6:69).

"The holy one of the Lord"—only once* is this expression found in the Old Testament. It is applied to Aaron, in whom holiness, as far as it could then be revealed, had found its most complete embodiment. The title waited for its fulfillment in Him who alone, in His own person, could perfectly show forth the holiness of God on earth—Jesus the Son of the Father. In Him we see holiness, as divine, as human, as our very own.

1. In Him we see wherein that incomparable excellence of the divine nature consists. "Thou lovest righteousness, and hatest iniquity, therefore God, even thy God, hath anointed thee with the oil of gladness above thy fellows." God's infinite hatred of sin and His maintenance of the right might appear to have little moral worth, as being a necessity of His nature. In the Son we see divine holiness tested. He is tried and tempted. He suffers, being tempted. He proves that holiness has indeed a moral worth: it is ready to make any sacrifice, even to give up life and cease to be, rather than consent to sin. In giving himself to die rather than yield to

---

*Ps. 106:6—margin of Authorized Version.

the temptation of sin and in giving himself to die that the Father's righteous judgment may be honored, Jesus proved how righteousness is an element of the divine holiness, and how the Holy One is sanctified in righteousness.

But this is only one side of holiness. The fire that consumes also purifies: it makes partakers of its own beautiful light-nature all that are capable of assimilation. So divine holiness not only maintains its own purity; it communicates it too. Herein was Jesus indeed seen to be the Holy One of God—that He never said, "Stand by, for I am holier than thou." His holiness proved itself to be the very incarnation of Him who had spoken, "Thus saith the high and lofty One . . . whose name is Holy; I dwell in the high and holy place, with him also that is of a contrite spirit" (Isa. 57:15). In Him was seen the affinity holiness has for all that are lost and helpless and sinful. He proved that holiness is not only the energy which in holy anger separates itself *from* all that are impure, but which in holy love separates *to* itself even the most sinful, to save and to bless. In Him we see how the divine holiness is the harmony of infinite righteousness with infinite love.

2. Such is the divine aspect of the character of Christ as He shows in human form what God's holiness is. But there is another aspect no less interesting and important to us. We not only want to know how God is holy, but how man must act in order to be holy as God is holy. Jesus came to teach us that it is possible to be men and yet to have the life of God dwelling in us. We ordinarily think that the glory and the infinite perfection of Deity are the proper setting in which the beauty of holiness is to be seen, but Jesus proved the perfect adaptation and suitability of human nature for showing forth that which is the essential glory of Deity. He showed us how—in choosing and doing the will of God and making it His own will—man may truly be holy as God is holy.

The value of this aspect of the Incarnation depends upon our full realization of the true humanity of our Lord. Because of the awful separating and purifying process that is always being carried on in the fiery furnace of the divine holiness, ever consuming and ever assimilating, we expect to see in Him the struggles of a truly human will. Holiness, to be truly human, must not only be a gift but an acquirement. Coming from God, it must be accepted and personally appropriated in the voluntary surrender of all that is not in accordance with it. In Jesus, as He distinctly gave up His own will and did and suffered the Father's will, we have the revelation of what human holiness is, and how truly man through the unity of will can be holy as God is holy.

3. But how does it help us to have seen in Jesus that a man can be holy? His example would only be a mockery if He could not show us the way and give us the power to become like himself. To accomplish this for us was indeed the supreme object of the Incarnation. The divine nature of Christ did not simply make *His* humanity partaker of its holiness, leaving Him still nothing more than an individual man. His divinity gave the human holiness He wrought out, the holy human nature which He perfected, an infinite value and power of communication. With Him a new life, the eternal life, was grafted into the stem of humanity. For all who believe in Him, He sanctified himself that they themselves might also be sanctified in truth. Because His death was the great triumph of His obedience to the will of the Father, it broke forever the dominion of sin, it atoned for our guilt, and won for Him from the Father the power to make His people partakers of His own life and holiness. In His resurrection and ascension the power of the new life and its right to universal dominion were made manifest. He is now in truth the Holy One of God, holding in himself as head the power of a holiness, at once divine and human, to communicate to every member of His body.

The Holy One of God—In a fullness of meaning that is beyond our understanding in spirit and in truth, Jesus now bears this title. He is now the one Holy One whom God sees, of such an infinite compass and power of holiness that He can be holiness to each of His brethren. Just as He is to God the Holy One, in whom God delights and for whose sake He delights in all who are in Christ, even so now Christ may be to us too the only Holy One in whom we delight, in whom the holiness of God has become ours. "We have believed and know that thou art the Holy One of God." Blessed are they who can say this and know themselves to be holy in Christ.

In speaking of the mystery of the Holy Trinity, we saw how Christ stands midway between the Father and the Spirit, as the point of union in which they meet. In the Son, "the express image of his person" (Heb. 1:3), we have the objective revelation of Deity, the divine holiness embodied and brought nigh. In the Holy Spirit we have the same revelation subjectively, the divine holiness entering our inmost being and revealing itself there. The work of the Holy Spirit is to reveal and glorify Christ as the Holy One of God, as He takes of His holiness and makes it ours. He shows us how all is in Christ, how Christ is all for us, how we are in Christ. He shows how, as a living Savior, Christ through His Spirit takes and keeps charge of us and our life of holiness. He makes Christ indeed to be to us the Holy One of God.

Do you want to be holy? Do you want to know God's way of holiness—learn to know Christ as the Holy One of God? In Him, you are "holy in Christ." By an act of divine power, you have been placed in Christ, and that same power keeps you there, planted and rooted in that divine fullness of life and holiness which there is in Him. This holy presence and the power of His eternal life, surround you. Let the Holy Spirit reveal this to you. The Holy Spirit is within you as the power of Christ and His life. Secretly, silently, but mightily, if you look to the Father for His working, He will strengthen the faith that you are in Christ, and that the divine life, which encircles you on every side, will enter in and take possession of you. Study and pray to believe and understand that it is in Christ as the Holy One of God, in Christ in whom the holiness of God is prepared for you for a holy nature and holy living, that you are, and there you may continue to abide.

Remember, this Christ is your Savior, the most patient and compassionate of teachers. Study holiness in the light of His countenance, looking up into His face. He came from heaven for the very purpose of making you holy. His love and power are more than your slowness and sinfulness. Recognize holiness as the inheritance prepared for you, as the power of a new life which Jesus waits and lives to dispense. Think of it as all in Him, and of its possession as being dependent upon the possession of himself. Even the disciples—although they scarcely understood what they confessed to believe, or where the Lord was leading them—even they became His saints, His holy ones because of their intense attachment to Him. So you, too, will find that to love Jesus fervently and obey Him simply is the sure path to holiness and the fullness of the Holy Spirit.

Prayer

Most Holy Lord God! I bless you that your beloved Son, whom you sanctified and sent into the world, is now to us the Holy One of God. I beseech you that my inner life may so be enlightened by the Spirit that I may in faith fully know what this means.

May I know Him as the revelation of your holiness, the incarnation in human nature, even unto the death, of your infinite and unconquerable hatred of sin, as of your amazing love to the sinner. May my soul be filled with great fear and trust of you.

May I know Him as the exhibition of the holiness in which we are now to walk before you. He lived in your holy will. May I know Him as He worked out that holiness, to be communicated to us in a new human nature, making it possible for us to live a holy life.

May I know Him as you have placed me in Him in heaven, holy in Christ, and as I may abide in Him by faith.

May I know Him, as He dwells in me, the Holy One of God on the throne of my heart, breathing His Holy Spirit and maintaining His holy rule. So shall I live holy in Christ.

O my Father, it pleased you that in your Son should all fullness dwell. In Him are hidden all the treasures of wisdom and knowledge; in Him dwell the unsearchable riches of grace and holiness. I beseech you, reveal Him to me, reveal Him in me, that I may not have to be satisfied with thoughts and desires, without the reality, but that in the power of an endless life I may know Him, and be known of Him, the Holy One of God. Amen.

Personal Application

1. In the holiness of Jesus we see what ours must be: righteousness that hates sin and gives everything to have it destroyed; love that seeks the sinner and gives everything to have him saved. "Whosoever doeth not righteousness is

not of God, neither he that loveth not his brother."

2. It is a solemn thought that we may be studying earnestly to know what holiness is but still have little of it, because we have little of Jesus. It is a blessed thought that a man may directly be little occupied with the thought of holiness, and yet have much of it, because he is full of Jesus.

3. We need the whole of what God teaches in His Word in regard to holiness in all its different aspects. We need still more to be ever returning to the living center where God imparts holiness. Jesus is the Holy One of God: to have Him truly, to love Him fervently, to trust and obey Him, to be in Him—this makes us holy.

4. Your holiness is thus treasured up in this divine, almighty, and most gentle Savior—surely there need be no fear that He will not be ready or able to make you holy.

5. With such a sanctifier, how does it happen that so many seekers after holiness fail so sadly, and know so little of the joy of a holy life?

I am sure with very many it is for one reason: they seek to grasp and hold this Christ in their own strength, and know not how that it is the Holy Spirit within who must be waited for to reveal this divine being, the Holy One of God, in their hearts.

CHAPTER FIFTEEN

The Holy Spirit

"But this spake he of the Spirit, which they that believe on him should receive: for the holy Spirit was not yet: because that Jesus was not yet glorified" (John 7:39).

"The Comforter, which is the Holy Ghost, whom the Father will send in my name, he shall teach you all things" (John 14:26).

"God hath from the beginning chosen you to salvation through sanctification of the Spirit and belief of the truth" (2 Thess. 2:13).

It has sometimes been said, that while the holiness of God stands out more prominently in the Old Testament, in the New it has to give way to the revelation of His love. The remark could hardly be made if it were fully realized that the Spirit is God, and that when He uses Holy as His own proper name, it is to teach us that now the holiness of God is to come nearer than ever, and to be clearly revealed as the power that makes us holy. In the Holy Spirit, God the Holy One of Israel and He who was the Holy One of God, comes close to fulfill the promise, "I am the Lord that make you holy." The unseen and unapproachable holiness of God had been revealed and brought near in the life of Christ Jesus; all that hindered our participation in it had been removed by His death. The name of Holy Spirit teaches us that it is particularly the work of the Spirit to impart holiness to us and make it our own.

Try and realize the meaning of this: the expression that through the whole Old Testament has belonged to the Holy

God is now appropriated to that Spirit which is within you. The holiness of God in Christ becomes holiness in you because this Spirit is in you. The words, Holy and Spirit, and the divine realities which they express, are now inseparably and eternally united. You can only have as much of the Spirit as you are willing to have of holiness. You can only have as much holiness as you have of the indwelling Spirit.

Some pray for the Spirit because they long to have His light and joy and strength, but their prayers bring little increase of blessing or power. It is because they do not rightly know or desire Him as the Holy Spirit. His burning purity, His searching and convicting light, His putting to death the deeds of the body, of self with its will and its power, His leading into the fellowship of Jesus as He gave up His will and His life to the Father—all this they do not know. The Spirit cannot work in power in them because they receive Him not as the Holy Spirit, in sanctification of the Spirit. At times, in seasons of revival, as among the Corinthians and Galatians, He may indeed come with His gifts and mighty workings, while His sanctifying power is but little manifest.* But unless that sanctifying power be acknowledged and accepted, His gifts will be lost. His gifts coming on us are only meant to prepare the way for the sanctifying power within us. We must take the lesson to heart; we can have as much of the Spirit as we are willing to have of His holiness. To be full of the Spirit must mean, Be fully holy.

The converse is equally true. We can have only as much holiness as we have of the Spirit. Some souls do earnestly seek to be holy, but it is largely in their own strength. They will read books and listen carefully to sermons; they will expend much effort to grasp every thought, and practice what they hear. Even so they must confess that they are still virtual strangers to the true, deep rest and joy and power of abiding in Christ and being holy in Him. They sought for holiness more than for the Spirit. They must learn how even all the holiness which is so near and clear in Christ is beyond our reach unless the Holy Spirit dwells within and imparts it. They must learn to pray for Him and His mighty strengthening (Eph. 3:16), to believe for Him (John 4:14; 7:37), in

---

*1 Cor. 3:1–3; 13:8; 14:4; Gal. 3:3; 5:15–26.

faith to yield to Him as indwelling (1 Cor. 3:14; 6:19). They must learn to cease from self-effort in thinking and believing, in willing and in running. They must hope in God, and wait patiently for Him. By His Holy Spirit He will make us holy. To be holy means, Be filled with the Spirit.

How is it that this Holy Spirit makes holy? The answer is—He reveals and imparts the holiness of Christ. Scripture tells us that Christ is made unto us sanctification. He sanctified himself for us that we ourselves might also be sanctified in truth. We have been sanctified through the offering of the body of Jesus Christ once for all. We are sanctified in Christ Jesus. The whole living Christ is just a treasury of holiness for man. In His life on earth He exchanged the divine holiness He possessed for the current coin needed for this human earthly life, humility, love, and obedience to the Father. As God, He has a sufficiency of all that is needed for every moment of the life of every believer.

But all this is beyond our reach, except as the Holy Spirit brings it to us and inwardly communicates it. However, this is the very work for which He bears the divine name, the Holy Spirit—to glorify Jesus, the Holy One of God, within us and so make us partakers of His holiness by revealing Christ, so that we begin to see what is in Him. He does it by unmasking the deep unholiness of our nature (Rom. 7:14–23). He mightily strengthens us to believe and receive Jesus himself as our life. He does it by leading us to utter despair of self, to absolute surrender of obedience to Jesus as Lord and to the assured confidence of faith in the power of an indwelling Christ. He does it by imparting the dispositions and graces of Christ in the secret silent depths of the heart and life, so that from the inner center of our life which has been renewed and sanctified in Christ, holiness should flow out to the utmost circumference and pervade all. Where desire has been awakened, and delight in the law of God has been created in the inner man, there—as the Spirit of this life in Christ Jesus—He sets us free from the law of sin and death in our members and leads us into the glorious liberty of the sons of God. As God within us, He communicates what God in Christ has prepared.

How do we obtain the working of this Holy Spirit who thus makes holy? The answer is very simple and clear. He is the Spirit of the Holy Father and of Christ, the Holy One of God: from them He must be received. "He showed me a river of water of life proceeding out of the throne of God and the Lamb." Jesus speaks of "the Holy Spirit, whom the Father will send in my name." He taught us to ask the Father. Paul prays for the Ephesians: "I bow my knees to the Father, that he may grant unto you, according to the riches of his glory, that ye may be strengthened with might by his Spirit in the inner man." As we look to God in His holiness and all its revelation from creation on, we see how the Spirit now flows out from the throne of His holiness as the water of life. Thus our hope is awakened to believe that God will have Him work mightily in us. We then see Jesus revealing that holiness in human nature, rending the veil in His atoning death that the Spirit from the holiest of all may come forth and as the Holy Spirit be Jesus' representative, thus making Him present within us. Seeing this, we become confident that faith in Jesus will bring the fullness of the Spirit.

Just as He told us to ask the Father, He told us to believe in himself. "He that believeth in me, rivers of living water shall flow out of him." Bow to the Father in the name of Christ, His Son; believe very simply in the Son as Him in whom the Father's love and blessing reach us. Then we may be assured that the Spirit, who is already within us as the Holy Spirit, will do His work in ever-increasing power. The mystery of holiness is the mystery of the Trinity: as we bow to the Father, believing in the Son, the Holy Spirit will work. Then we shall see the true meaning of what God spake in Israel: "I am holy," thus speaks the Father; "Be holy," as my Son and in my Son; "I make holy," through the Spirit of my Son dwelling in you. Let our souls worship and cry out, "Holy, holy, holy is the Lord God of hosts."

The Holy Spirit: All true knowledge and all participation in holiness—the Father's, which inspires adoration, and the Son's, which is meant to be ours—depend upon our life in the Spirit and upon our knowing and acknowledging Him as abiding in us as our life. What stands in the way that the holiness of such a Thrice Holy God does not extend to more of His Church and His children? The Holy Spirit is among us, is in us—it must be we grieve and resist Him. If you would remove this hindrance, bow before the Father without delay, that He may grant you the Spirit's mighty working in the inner man. Believe that the Holy Spirit, bearer to you of all the holiness of God and of Jesus, is indeed within you. Let Him take the place of self with its thoughts and efforts. In holy silence, quiet your soul before God for Him to give you wisdom. Rest, in emptiness and poverty of spirit, in the faith that He will work in His own way. Just as the holiness that Jesus brings is divine, so is the power in which the Holy Spirit communicates it. Yield yourself day by day in growing dependence and obedience to wait on and be led of Him. Let the fear of the Holy One be on you. Sanctify the Lord God in your heart; let Him be your fear and dread. Fear not only sin; above all fear self, as it boldly thrusts itself before God with its service. Let self die by refusing and denying its work. Let the Holy Spirit—in quietness and dependence, in the surrender of obedience and trust—have the rule, the free disposal of every faculty. Wait for Him—in power He can, He will, reveal and impart the holiness of the Father and the Son.*

Prayer

Holy, holy, holy, Lord God of hosts, the whole earth is full of your glory! Let that glory fill the heart of your child as he bows before you. I come to drink of the river of the water of life that flows from under the throne of God and of the Lamb. Glory be to God and to the Lamb for the gift that hath not entered into the heart of man to conceive—the gift of the Holy indwelling Spirit.

O my Father, in the name of Jesus I ask that I may be strengthened with might by your Spirit in my inmost self. Help me to believe that you have given Him, and help me to accept and expect Him to fill and rule my whole inner being. Teach me to surrender to Him, not to will or run, not to think or work in my strength, but in quiet confidence to wait and

---

*I feel deeply that one lack among believers is that they do not know the Holy Spirit, who is within them. Thereby they lose the blessed life He would work in them. If it please God, I hope that the next volume of this series may be on *The Spirit of Christ*. May the Father give me a message that shall help His children to know what the Holy Spirit can be to them.

know that He works in me. Teach me what it is to have no confidence in the flesh and to serve you in the Spirit. Teach me what it is in all things to be led by your Holy Spirit, the Spirit of your holiness.

Gracious Father, grant that through Him I may hear you speak and reveal yourself to me in power: I am holy. May He glorify Jesus to me and in me, Jesus in whom your command "Be holy" has been so blessedly fulfilled on my behalf. Let the Holy Spirit give me the anointing and the sealing which bring the perfect assurance that in Him your promise is being gloriously fulfilled, "I make you holy." Amen.

Personal Application

1. It is universally admitted that the Holy Spirit has not, in the teaching of the Church or the faith of believers, that place of honor and power which are due to Him as the revealer of the Father and the Son. Seek a deep conviction that without the Holy Spirit the clearest teaching on holiness, the most fervent desires, the most blessed experiences even, will only be temporary, will produce no permanent result, will bring no abiding rest.

2. The Holy Spirit dwells within, and works within, in the hidden deep of your nature. Seek above everything the clear and constant assurance that He is within you, doing His work.

3. To this end, deny self and its work in serving God. Your own power to think and pray and believe and strive—one by one lay this all down in God's presence; claim, accept, and believe in the hidden workings of the indwelling Spirit.

4. As the Son always spoke of the Father, so the Spirit always points to Christ. The soul that yields itself to the Spirit will learn of Him to know how Christ is our holiness, how we can always abide in Christ our sanctification. What a vain effort it has often been without the Spirit! "As the anointing taught you, ye abide in him."

5. Believer, in the temple of your heart, there is a secret place within the veil where the Spirit of God dwells—often unrecognized. Bow in deep reverence before the Father and ask that He may work mightily. Expect the Spirit to do His work: He will make your inner man a fit home and your heart a throne for Jesus, and will reveal Him there.

CHAPTER SIXTEEN

Holiness and Truth

"Sanctify them through thy truth: thy word is truth" (John 17:17).
*"God hath . . . chosen you to salvation through sanctification of
the Spirit and belief of the truth"* (2 Thess. 2:13).

The chief means of sanctification that God uses is His
Word. And yet how much reading and studying, teaching
and preaching of the Word has almost no effect in making
men holy. It is not the Word that sanctifies; God alone can
sanctify. Nor is it simply through the Word that God does it,
but through truth which is in the Word. As a means the word
is of unspeakable value, as the vessel which contains the
truth—*if God use it.* As a means it is of no value if God does
not use it. Strive to connect God's Holy Word with the holy
God himself. God sanctifies in the truth through His Word.

Jesus had just said, "The words which thou gavest me, I
have given them." Do we realize what that means? Think of
that great transaction in eternity: the Infinite Being whom
we call God giving His words to His Son; in His words opening up His heart, communicating His mind and will, revealing himself and all His purpose and love. In a divine power
and reality beyond our imagination, God gave Christ His
words. In the same living power Christ gave His disciples
those words—full of divine life and energy to work in their
hearts as they were able to receive them. Just as in the words
of a man on earth we expect to find all the wisdom or all the

goodness there is in him, so the word of the Thrice Holy One is vitally alive with the holiness of God. All the holy fire—His burning zeal and His burning love—dwells in His words.

But men can handle these words, study and say them, and still be complete strangers to their holiness or their power to make holy. God himself, the Holy One, must be the one to produce holiness through the Word. Every seed, in which the life of a tree is contained, is encircled by a husk or shell which protects and hides the inner life. Only where the seed finds congenial soil and the husk is burst and removed can the seed germinate and grow. And only where there is a heart in harmony with God's holiness, longing for it, yielding itself to it, will the word really make holy. The heart that is not content with the word but seeks the living, holy One in the Word, to that heart He will reveal the truth, and in it himself. It is the word—given to us by Christ as God gave it to Him, and received by us as it was by Him to rule and fill our life—that has power to make holy.

But we must notice especially how our Savior says, Sanctify them, not in the word but in the truth. Just as in man there is body, soul, and spirit, so in truth too. First there is word-truth: a man may have the correct form of words while he does not really apprehend the truth they contain. Then there is thought-truth: there may be a clear intellectual apprehension of truth without the experience of its power. The Bible speaks of truth as a living reality—this is the life-truth, in which the very Spirit of truth we profess has entered and possessed our inner being. Christ calls himself the truth: He is said to be full of grace and truth. The divine life and grace are in Him as an actual, substantial existence and reality. He not only acts upon us by thoughts and motives, but communicates as a reality the eternal life He brought for us from the Father. The Holy Spirit is called the Spirit of truth; what He imparts is real, actual, the very substance of unseen things. He guides into the truth, not thought-truth or doctrine only, but life-truth, the personal possession of the truth as it is in Jesus. As the Spirit of truth He is the Spirit of holiness. The life of God, which is His holiness, He brings to us an actual possession.

It is now of this living truth, which dwells in the Word as the seed-life dwells in the husk, that Jesus says, "Make them holy in the truth: thy word is truth." He would have us mark the intimate connection, as well as the wide difference, between the Word and the truth. The connection is one willed by God and meant to be inseparable. "Thy word is truth"; with God they are one—but not with man. There were men in close contact and continual fellowship with Jesus to whom He was only a man and nothing more. Just so there are Christians who know and understand the Word and yet are strangers to its true spiritual power. They have the letter but not the spirit. The truth comes to them in word but not in power. The Word does not make them holy, because they hold it not in spirit and in truth. On the contrary, there are others who receive and love the truth, who in all their dealings with the Word, yield themselves to the Spirit of truth who dwells in it and in them too. To these the Word comes indeed as truth, as a divine reality, communicating and working that of which it speaks of. It is of such use of the Word that the Savior says, "Make them holy in the truth: thy word is truth." Just as the words which God gave Him were all in the power of the eternal life, love and will of God, revealing and communicating the Father's purpose, and just as God's Word was truth to Him and in Him, so it can be in us. When we thus receive it, we are made holy in the truth.

What lessons are here for the path of holiness? First, be sure that in all our contacts with God's blessed Word, we rest content with nothing short of experiencing it as the truth of God, as spirit and as power. Jesus said, "If ye abide in my word, ye shall know the truth." No analysis can ever find or prove the life of a seed. Plant it in its proper soil, and growth will testify to the life. Only as the Word of God is received in love as it grows and works in us, can we know its truth, and be sure that it is the truth of God. As we live in the words of Jesus, in love and obedience, keeping and doing them, then the truth from heaven—the power of the divine life which there is in them—will reveal itself to us. Christ is the truth; in Him the love and grace, the very life of God, has come to earth as an existence with substance, a living, mighty power, something new that never was on earth before (John 1:17). Let us yield ourselves to the living Christ to possess us and to rule us as the living truth, then will God's Word be truth to us and in us.

The Spirit of Christ is the Spirit of truth. That actual heavenly reality of divine life and love in Christ, the truth, has a Spirit, who comes to communicate and impart it. Beware of trying to study or understand or even to take possession of God's Word without that Spirit through whom the Word was spoken of old. Without it we shall find only the husk. The truth or thought and sentiment may be very beautiful perhaps but have no power to make us holy. We must have the Spirit of truth within us. He will lead us into the truth; when we are in the truth, God makes us holy in it and by it. The truth must be in us, and we in it. God desires truth in the inward parts. Christ says, "If ye were of the truth" and "he that is of the truth knoweth me"—we must be people like this. In daily life and conduct, in thought and action, even in this lower sphere, there must be an intense love of truth and a willingness to sacrifice everything for it. In the spiritual life, there must be a deep hungering to have all our religion every day, every moment, stand fully in the truth of God. To the simple, humble, childlike spirit, the truth of the Word will be unsealed and revealed. In such the Spirit of truth comes to dwell. In such, as they daily wait before the Holy One in silence and emptiness, in reverence and holy fear, His Holy Spirit works and gives the truth within. In thus imparting Christ as revealed in the Word, in His divine life and love as their own life, He makes them holy with the holiness of Christ.

Another lesson lies in that prayer, the earthly echo of the prayer which He ever lives to pray, "Holy Father, make them holy in the truth." Would you be holy, child of God? Cast yourself into that mighty current of intercession ever flowing into, ever reaching, the Father's bosom. Be borne upon it until your whole soul cries with unutterable groanings, too deep and intense for human speech, "Holy Father, make me holy in the truth." Then trusting in Christ as the truth and reality of what you desire and trusting in His all-prevailing intercession, as you wait for the Spirit within as the Spirit of truth, look up to the Father—expect His own direct and almighty working to make you holy. The mystery of holiness is the mystery of the Triune One. The deeper entrance into the holy life rests in the fellowship of the Three in One. It is the Father who establishes us in Christ, who gives each day anew of the Holy Spirit. To the Holy Father the soul must look up continually in the prayer, "Make me holy in the truth."

In the word *holy* we have the central thought of the high-priestly prayer. As the Father's attribute (John 17:11), as the Son's work for himself and us (v. 19), as the direct work of the Father through the Spirit (vv. 17, 20)—all reveal the glory of God in himself and in us. Let us enter into the holiest of all and bow with our great High Priest. Then let the deep, unceasing cry go up for all the Church of God, "Holy Father, make them holy in the truth: thy word is truth!" The word in which God makes holy is summed up in this, *Holy in Christ.* May God make it truth to us!

Prayer

Blessed Father, you told Israel, "I the Lord am holy and make holy." But it is only in your beloved Son that the full glory of your holiness, as making us holy, has been revealed. You are our Holy Father. You make us holy in your truth.

We thank you that your Son has given us the words you gave Him, and that as He received them from you in life and power, we may receive them too. O Father! with our whole heart we do receive them. Let the Spirit make them truth and life within us. So shall we know you as the Holy One, consuming the sin, renewing the sinner.

We bless you most for your Blessed Son, the Holy One of God, the living Word in whom the truth dwelleth. We thank you that in His never-ceasing intercession, this cry ever reaches you, "Father, sanctify them in thy truth." We praise you that the answer is ever streaming forth from your glory. Holy Father, make us holy in your truth, in your wonderful revelation of yourself in Him who is the truth. Let your Holy Spirit have dominion in our hearts so that by Jesus sanctifying himself for us, we may be sanctified in the truth. May He be to us the way, the truth, and the life. May we know that in Him we are in your presence and that our answer to our prayer to make us holy is—Holy in Christ. Amen.

Personal Application

1. God is the God of truth—not truth in speaking only or truth of doctrine—but truth of existence, or life in its divine

reality. And Christ is the truth; the actual embodiment of this divine life. There is a kingdom of truth, of divine spiritual realities, of which Christ is King. And the very essence of all this truth of God in Christ is the Spirit. He is the Spirit of truth. He leads us into it, so that we are of the truth and walk in it. The reality there is in God—holiness—is the deepest root of the truth; the Spirit of truth is the Holy Spirit.

2. It is the work of the Father to make us holy in the truth. Let us bow very low in childlike trust as we pray, "Holy Father, make us holy in the truth." He will do it.

3. It is the intercession of the Son that asks and obtains this blessing. Let us take our place in Him, and rejoice in the assurance of an answer.

4. It is the Spirit of truth through whom the Father does this work, so that we may dwell in the truth and the truth in us. Let us yield freely and fully to the leading of the Spirit, in our dealing with God's Word, so that as the Son prays, the Father may make us holy in the truth.

5. In the light of the Three-One, let us never read the Word except with this aim: to be made holy in the truth by God.

CHAPTER SEVENTEEN

Holiness and Crucifixion

"For their sakes I sanctify myself, that they also may be sanctified through the truth" (John 17:19).

"Then said he, Lo, I come to do thy will. . . . By the which will we are sanctified through the offering of the body of Jesus Christ once for all. For by one offering he hath perfected for ever them that are sanctified" (Heb. 10:9, 10, 14).

In His high-priestly prayer on His way to Gethsemane and Calvary, Jesus said to the Father: "I sanctify myself." Not long before He had spoken of himself as "the Son whom the Father hath sanctified and sent into the world." From Scripture we are familiar with the thought that, what God has sanctified, man has to sanctify too. The work of the Father in sanctifying the Son is the basis and groundwork of the work of the Son in sanctifying himself. If His holiness as man was to be a free and personal possession, accepted and assimilated in voluntary and conscious self-determination, it was not enough that the Father sanctify Him; He must sanctify himself too.

This self-sanctifying of our Lord took place through His whole life, but culminates and comes out with special clarity in His crucifixion. Wherein it consists is explained in Hebrews. The Messiah said, "Lo, I come to do thy will." And then it is added, "By the which will we are sanctified through the offering of the body of Christ." It was the offering of the body of Christ that was the will of God; in doing that will He sanctified us. About the doing of His Father's will in the offering His body He said, "I sanctify myself, that they themselves also may be sanctified in truth." Giving up His will to God's will in the agony of Gethsemane, and then doing that will in obedience unto death, was Christ's sanctifying himself and us too.

The holiness of God is revealed in His will. Holiness even in the Divine Being has no moral value except as it is freely willed. In speaking of the Trinity, theologians have pointed out how, as the Father represents the absolute necessity of everlasting goodness, the Son proves its liberty: within the Divine Being it is willed in love. And this now was the work of the Son on earth, amid the trials and temptations of a human life, to accept and hold fast at any sacrifice, and with His whole heart to will the will of the Father.

"Though he were a Son, yet learned he obedience by the things which he suffered." In Gethsemane the conflict between the will of human nature and the divine will reached its height—it manifests itself in language which almost makes us tremble for his sinlessness as He speaks of His will in antithesis to God's will. But the struggle is a victory because, clearly conscious of what it would mean to have His own will, He surrenders it and says, "Thy will be done." To enter into the will of God He gives up His very life. In His crucifixion He thus reveals the law of sanctification. Holiness is the full entrance of our will into God's will. Or rather, holiness is the entrance of God's will to be the death of our will. The only end of our will and deliverance from it is death to it under the righteous judgment of God. In the surrender to the death of the cross Christ sanctified himself, and sanctified us, that we also might be sanctified in truth.

Now, just as the Father sanctified Him, and He in virtue thereof appropriated it and sanctified himself, so we, whom He has sanctified, have to appropriate it to ourselves. In no other way than crucifixion, the giving up of himself to the death, could Christ realize the sanctification He had from the Father. And in no other way can we realize the sanctification we have in Him. His and our sanctification bear the common stamp of the cross.

We have seen before that obedience is the path to holiness. In Christ we see that the path to perfect holiness is perfect obedience. That means obedience unto death, even to the giving up of life, even the death of the cross. The sanctification which Christ wrought for us, offering His body, bears the death mark and we cannot partake of it either except as we die to self and its will. Crucifixion is the path to sanctification.

This lesson is in harmony with all we have seen. The first revelation of God's holiness to Moses was accompanied with the command: "Put off." God's praise, as glorious in holiness, fearful in praises, was sounded over the dead bodies of the Egyptians. When Moses on Sinai was commanded to sanctify the Mount, it was said, "If any touch it, man or beast, it shall not live." *The holiness of God is death to all that is in contact with sin.* Only through death, through blood-shedding, was there access to the holiest of all. Christ chose death, even death as a curse, that He might sanctify himself for us, and open to us the path to holiness, to the holiest of all, to the Holy One. It is still the same today.

No man can see God and live. Only in death, the death of self and of nature, can we draw near and behold God. Christ led the way. No man can see God and live. "Then let me die, Lord," one has cried, "but see Thee I must!" So real is this right that Christ gives us and so genuine our union to Him that we may live in His death; as self is kept in the place of death day by day, the life and the holiness of Christ can be ours.

Where is the place of death? How can the crucifixion which leads to holiness and to God be accomplished in us? Thank God! it is through no work of our own, no weary process of self-crucifixion. The crucifixion that is to sanctify us is an accomplished fact. The cross bears the banner, "It is finished." On it Christ sanctified himself for us that we might be sanctified in truth. Our crucifixion, like our sanctification, is something that in Christ has been completely and perfectly finished. "We have been sanctified through the offering of the body of Jesus Christ once for all." "By one offering he hath perfected for ever them that are sanctified." In that fullness, which it is the Father's good pleasure should dwell in Christ, the crucifixion of our old man, of the flesh, of the world, of ourselves, is all a spiritual reality. He that desires and knows and accepts Christ, fully receives all this in Him.

Christ had previously been known especially for His pardoning, quickening, and saving grace. Now as He is sought again in the role of a real deliverer from the power of sin—as a sanctifier—He comes and includes the soul in the fellowship of the sacrifice of His will. "He put away sin by the sacrifice of himself" must become true of us as it is of Him. He reveals how it is part of His salvation to make us partakers of a will entirely surrendered to the will of God, of a life that had yielded itself to death, and then had been given back from the dead by the power of God—a life of which the crucifixion of self-will was the spirit and the power. He reveals this. The soul that sees and consents to it, that yields its will and its life and believes in Jesus as its death and life, and in His crucifixion as its possession and its inheritance, enters into the enjoyment and experience of it—*now*. "I died that I might live: I have been crucified with Christ, and it is no longer I that live, but Christ that liveth in me." The life it now lives is by faith in the Son of God, the daily acceptance in faith of Him who lives within us in the power of a death that has been passed through and forever finished.

"I sanctify myself for them, that they themselves also may be sanctified in truth." "I come to do thy will, O God. By the which will," the will of God accomplished by Christ, "we are sanctified through the one offering of the body of Christ." Christ's giving up His will in Gethsemane and accepting God's will in dying; Christ's doing that will in obedience to the death of the cross, this is His sanctifying himself, and this is our being sanctified in truth. The death to self, the utter, absolute giving up of our own life with its will and power and aims to the cross and into the crucifixion of Christ, the daily bearing the cross—not a cross on which we are yet to be crucified, but the cross of the crucified Christ with power to kill and make dead—this is the secret of the life of holiness; this is true sanctification.

Is this the holiness which you are seeking? Do you see, do you agree that God alone is holy, that self is unholy, and that there is no way to be made holy except by the fire of divine holiness coming in to put self to death? "Always bearing about in the body the dying of Jesus, that the life also of Jesus may be manifested in our mortal body"—is the pathway for each one who truly seeks to be sanctified, even as He was.

Jesus sanctified himself for us that we ourselves also might be sanctified in truth. Yes, our sanctification rests and roots in His, in Him. And we are in Him. The secret roots of our being are planted into Jesus. Deeper down than we can see or feel, there is He our vine, bearing and quickening us. In a way and to a degree which are far beyond our comprehension, intensely divine and real, we are in Him who sanctified himself for us. Let us dwell there, where we have been placed of God. Let us pray to the Father to mightily strengthen us by His Spirit that Christ as our sanctification may dwell in our hearts, that the power of His death and His life may be revealed in us, and God's will be done in us as it was in Him.

Prayer

Holy Father! I bless you for this blessed word and the work of your beloved Son. In His never-ceasing intercession you always hear the prayer, "I sanctify myself for them, that they themselves also may be sanctified in truth."

Strengthen me by your Spirit so that in faith I may accept and live the holiness prepared for me in my Lord Jesus. Give me spiritual understanding to know what it means that He sanctified himself, that my sanctification is secured in His, that as by faith I abide in Him, its power will cover my whole life. Let His sanctification indeed be the law as it is the life of mine. Let His surrender to your fatherly will, His continual dependence and obedience, be its root and its strength. Let His death to the world and to sin be its daily rule. O my Father, above all let the living Jesus, who was sanctified for me, be my only trust and stay. He sanctified himself for me that I myself may be sanctified in truth.

Beloved Savior, how shall I rightly bless and love and glorify you for this wondrous grace! You gave yourself so that now I am holy in you. I give myself that in you I myself may be made holy in truth. Amen. Lord Jesus! Amen.

Personal Application

1. "If any man would come after me, let him deny himself, and take up his cross, and follow me." Jesus means that

our life shall be the exact counterpart of His, including even the crucifixion. The beginning of such a life is the denial of self, to give Christ its place. The Jews would not deny self, but "denied the Holy One . . . and killed the Prince of Life." The choice is still between Christ and self. Let us deny the unholy one, and give him to the death.

2. The steps in this path are these: First, the deliberate decision that self shall be given up to the death; then the surrender to Christ crucified to make us partakers of His crucifixion; then, "knowing that our old man is crucified," the faith that says, "I am crucified with Christ"; and finally, the power to live as a crucified one, to glory in the cross of Christ.

3. This is God's way of holiness, a divine mystery, which the Holy Spirit alone can daily maintain in us. Blessed be God, it is the life which a Christian can live because Christ lives in us.

4. The central thought is: We are in Christ, who gave up His will and did the will of God. By the Holy Spirit the mind that was in Him is in us, the will of self is crucified, and we live in the will of God.

CHAPTER EIGHTEEN

Holiness and Faith

"That they may receive forgiveness of sins, and inheritance among them which are sanctified by faith . . . in me" (Acts 26:18).

The more we study Scripture in the light of the Holy Spirit or practice the Christian life in His power, the deeper becomes our conviction of the unique and central place faith has in God's plan of salvation. We see, too, that it is fitting and right that it should be so: the very nature of things demands it. Because God is a spiritual and invisible being, every revelation of Him, whether in His works, His Word, or His Son, calls for faith. Faith is the spiritual sense of the soul, being to it what the senses are to the body. By faith alone we enter into communication and contact with God.

Faith is that meekness of soul which waits in stillness to hear, understand and accept what God says, and to receive, retain, and possess what God gives or does. By faith we allow, we welcome God himself, the living person, to enter in to make His abode with us and become our very life. However well we think we know it, we always have to learn the truth afresh, to see a deeper and fuller application of it, that in the Christian life faith is the first thing—the one thing—that pleases God and brings blessing to us. And because holiness is God's highest glory and the highest blessing He has for us, it is especially in the life of holiness that we need to live by faith alone.

Our Lord speaks here of "them that are sanctified by faith in me."* He himself is our sanctification as He is our justification: for both it is faith that God asks, and both are equally given at once. The participle used here is not the present, denoting a process or work that is being carried on, but the aorist, indicating an act done once for all. When we believe in Christ, we receive the whole Christ, our justification and our sanctification: we are at once accepted by God as righteous in Him and as holy in Him. God counts and calls us what we really are—sanctified ones in Christ. As we are led to see what God sees and as our faith grasps that the holy life of Christ is ours in actual possession, to be accepted and appropriated for daily use, then we shall really be able to live the life God calls us to—the life of holy ones in Christ Jesus. We shall then be in the right position in which what is called our progressive sanctification can be worked out. It will be the acceptance and application in daily life of the power of a holy life which has been prepared in Jesus, which has in the union with Him become our present and permanent possession, and which works in us according to the measure of our faith.

From this point of view it is evident that faith has a twofold operation. Faith is the evidence of things not seen, though now actually existing, the substance of things hoped for, but not yet present. It deals with the unseen present as well as with the unseen future. As the evidence of things not seen, it rejoices in Christ our complete sanctification as a present possession. Through faith I simply look to what Christ is as revealed in the Word by the Holy Spirit. Claiming all He is as my own, I know that His holiness, His holy nature and life are mine; I am a holy one. By faith in Him I have been sanctified.

This is the first aspect of sanctification: it looks to what is a complete and finished thing, an absolute reality. As the substance of things hoped for, this faith reaches out in the

*The best commentators connect the expression "by faith in me" not with the word "sanctified," but with the whole clause, "that by faith in me they may receive." This will, however, in no way affect the application to the word "sanctified." Thus read, the text tells us that the remission of sin, and the inheritance, and the sanctification which qualifies for the inheritance, are all received by faith.

assurance of hope to the future, to things I do not yet see or experience, and claims day by day, out of Christ our sanctification, what it needs for practical holiness, "to be holy in all manner of living."

This is the second aspect of sanctification: in personal experience I depend upon Jesus to supply, gradually and unceasingly, for the need of each moment, all that has been treasured up in His fullness. "Of God are ye in Christ Jesus, who of God is made unto us sanctification."

Under its first aspect faith says, "I know I am in Him, and all His holiness is mine." In its second aspect it says, "I trust in Him for the grace and the strength I need each moment to live a holy life."

And yet it need hardly be said, these two are one. It is one Jesus who is our sanctification, whether we look at it in the light of what He is made for us once for all, or what, as the fruit of that, He becomes to our experience day by day. And so it is one faith which—the more it studies and adores and rejoices in Jesus as made of God unto us sanctification, as Him in whom we have been sanctified—becomes the bolder to expect the fulfillment of every promise for daily life, and the stronger to claim the victory over every sin. Faith in Jesus is the secret of a holy life. All holy conduct, all really holy deeds, are the fruit of faith in Jesus as our holiness.

We know how faith acts and what its great hindrances are in the matter of justification. It is well that we remind ourselves that there are the same dangers in the exercise of sanctifying as of justifying faith. Faith in God stands opposed to trust in self: especially to the willing and working of self. Faith is hindered by every effort to do something ourselves. Faith looks to God working and yields itself to His strength, as revealed in Christ through the Spirit. It allows God to work both to will and to do. Faith must work. Without works it is dead, by works alone can it be perfected. In Jesus Christ, as Paul says, nothing avails but "faith working by love." But these works, which faith in God's working inspires and performs, are very different from the works in which a believer often puts forth his best efforts, only to find that he fails. The true life of holiness, the life of them who are sanctified in Christ, has its root and its strength in an abiding sense of utter impotence, in the deep restfulness which trusts in the working of a divine power and life, in the entire personal surrender to the loving Savior in that faith which consents to be nothing that He may be all.

It may appear impossible to discern or describe the difference between the working that is of self and the working that is of Christ through faith: if we but know that there is such a difference, if we learn to distrust ourselves, and to count on Christ working, the Holy Spirit will lead us into this secret of the Lord too. Faith's works are Christ's works.

Just as faith is hindered by effort, so faith also is hindered by the desire to see and feel. "If thou believest, thou shalt see." The Holy Spirit will seal our faith with a divine experience; we shall see the glory of God. But this is His work. Ours is—when all appears dark and cold, in the face of all that nature or experience testifies—still to believe each moment in Jesus as our all-sufficient sanctification, in whom we are perfected before God. Complaints as to want of feeling, as to weakness or deadness, seldom profit. The soul that refused to be preoccupied with itself, either with its own weakness or the strength of the enemy, but who only looks to what Jesus is and has promised to do—to that soul progress in holiness will be a joyful march from victory to victory. "The Lord himself doth fight for you." This thought, so often repeated in connection with Israel's possession of the promised land, is the food of faith. In conscious weakness, in presence of mighty enemies, it sings the conqueror's song. When God appears to be not doing what we trusted Him for, then is just the time for faith to glory in Him.

Perhaps nothing more fully reveals the true character of faith than joy and praise. You promise a child a present tomorrow. At once he says, "thank you" and is glad. Joyful thanks are the proof that your promise was believed. You are told by a friend of a rich legacy he has left you in his will. It may not come true for years, but even now it makes you glad. We have already seen what an element of holiness joy is; it is especially an element of holiness by faith. How beautiful and how perfect God's provision is, by which my holiness is in Jesus and by which I am to allow Him to work in me. Each time I realize the truth of this, my heart ought to rise up in praise and thanks. Instead of thinking that this life of holiness through faith is a life of difficult attainment and continual self-denial, we ought to praise God exceedingly that He has made it possible and sure for us. We can be holy, because Jesus the mighty and the loving One is our holiness. Praise will express our faith; praise will prove it; praise will strengthen it. "Then believed they his words; they sang his praise." Praise will commit us to faith: we shall see that we have only one thing to do—to go on in a faith that ever trusts and ever praises. It is in a living, loving attachment to Jesus, that rejoices in Him and praises Him continually for what He is to us, that faith proves itself and receives the power of holiness.

"Sanctified by faith in me." It is the personal, living Jesus who offers himself in all the riches of His power and love as the object, the strength, the life of our faith. He tells us that if we would be always and in everything holy, we must see to only one thing: to be always and altogether full of faith in Him. Faith is the eye of the soul, the power by which we discern the presence of the Unseen One, as He comes to give himself to us. Faith not only sees but appropriates and assimilates. Let the Holy Spirit who dwells in us do that for which He has been given to us—quicken and strengthen faith. Faith is surrender, yielding ourselves to Jesus to allow Him to do His work in us, submitting ourselves to Him to live out His life and work out His will in us. Thus we shall find Him giving himself entirely to us and taking complete possession. So faith will be power, the power of obedience to do God's will. This is "our most holy faith," "the faith delivered to the holy ones." To the single-hearted, the secret of holiness is simple: Jesus. We are in Him, our sanctification. He personally is our holiness; and the life of faith in Him, that receives and possesses Him, must necessarily be a life of holiness. Jesus says, "Sanctified by faith in me."

Prayer

Beloved Lord, again I have seen, with adoring wonder, what you are willing to be to me. It is in you and a life of living fellowship with you, that I am to become holy. In the simple life of personal attachment, of trust and love, of surrender and consecration, you will become my all, and make me partaker of you and your holiness.

Blessed Lord Jesus, I do believe in you, help my unbelief. I confess what still remains of unbelief and count on your presence to conquer and cast it out. My soul sees more and more how you yourself are my life and my holiness. You enlarge my heart to rejoice in you as my all, and assure me that you yourself take possession and fill the temple of my being with your glory. You are teaching me that, however feeble and human and disappointing experiences may be, your Holy Spirit is the strength of my faith, leading me into a stronger and a deeper confidence in you in whom I am holy.

O my Savior, I take your word this day, "Sanctified by faith in me," as a new revelation of your love and its purpose with me. In you alone is the power of my holiness; in you is the power of my faith. Blessed be your name for giving me a place among them of whom you say: "Sanctified by faith in me." Amen.

Personal Application

1. Let us remember that it is not only the faith that is dealing particularly with Christ for sanctification, but all living faith, that has the power to sanctify. Anything that casts the soul wholly on Jesus, that calls forth intense and simple trust, whether the trial of faith or the prayer of faith or the work of faith, helps to make us holy, because it brings us into living contact with the Holy One.

2. It is only through the Holy Spirit that Christ and His holiness are day by day revealed and made ours in actual possession. And so the faith which receives Him is of the Spirit too. Yield yourself in simplicity and trust to His working. Do not be afraid, as if you cannot believe: you have "the Spirit of faith" within you: you have the power to believe. And you may ask God to strengthen you mightily by His Spirit in the inner man, for the faith that receives Christ in the indwelling that knows no break.

3. I have only as much faith as I have of the Spirit. Is not this then what I most need—to live entirely under the influence of the Spirit?

4. Just as the eye in seeing is receptive, and yields to let the object placed before it make its impression, so faith is the impression God makes on the soul when He draws nigh.

Was not the faith of Abraham the fruit of God's drawing near and speaking to him, the impression God made on him? Let us be still to gaze on the divine mystery of Christ our holiness: His presence, waited for and worshiped, will work the faith. That is, the Spirit that proceeds from Him into those who cling to Him will be faith.

5. Holiness by faith in Jesus, not the effort of thine own,
   Sin's dominion crushed and broken by the power of grace alone,
   God's own holiness within thee, His own beauty on thy brow—
   This shall be thy pilgrim brightness, this thy blessed portion now.

                                                    F.R.H.

CHAPTER NINETEEN

Holiness and Resurrection

"Concerning his Son Jesus Christ our Lord which was made of the seed of David according to the flesh; and declared to be the Son of God with power, according to the spirit of holiness, by the resurrection of the dead" (Rom. 1:3, 4).

These words speak of a twofold birth of Christ. According to the flesh, He was born of the seed of David. According to the Spirit, He was the first begotten from the dead. Just as He was a Son of David in virtue of His birth through the flesh, so He was declared to be the Son of God with power, in virtue of His resurrection birth through the Spirit of holiness. The life He received through His first birth was a life in and after the flesh with its weakness, but the new life He received in the resurrection was a life in the power of the Spirit of holiness.

The expression "the Spirit of holiness" is a peculiar one. Here the word used for God's holiness is not the same word as that used in Heb. 12:10, which describes holiness in the abstract as the attribute of an object, but another word (also used in 2 Cor. 7:1 and 1 Thess. 3:13) expressing the habit of holiness in its action—practical holiness or sanctity. Paul used this word, because He wished to emphasize the thought that Christ's resurrection was definitely the result of that life of holiness and self-sanctifying which had culminated in His death. It was the spirit of the life of holiness which He had lived, in the power of which He was raised again. He

127

teaches us that life and death of self-sanctification, in which alone our sanctification stands, was the root and ground of His resurrection and of its declaration that He was the Son of God with power, the first begotten from the dead. The resurrection was the fruit which that life of holiness bore.

And so the life of holiness becomes the property of all who are partakers of the resurrection. The resurrection life and the Spirit of holiness are inseparable. Christ sanctified himself in death that we ourselves might be sanctified in truth: when in virtue of the Spirit of sanctity He was raised from the dead, that Spirit of holiness was proved to be the power of resurrection life, and the resurrection life to be a life of holiness.

As a believer you have part in this resurrection life. You have been "begotten again by the resurrection of Jesus Christ from the dead." You are "risen with Christ." You are commanded "to reckon yourself to be alive unto God in Christ Jesus." But the life can work in power only as you seek to know it, to yield to it, and let it have full possession and mastery. And if it is to do this, one of the most important things to see is that, just as it was by virtue of the Spirit of holiness that Christ was raised, so also the Spirit of that same holiness must be in you the mark and the power of your life. Study to know and possess the Spirit of holiness as it was seen in the life of your Lord.

What was the secret of that holiness? The key lies here: "Lo, I am come to do thy will, O God." "By the which will," as done by Christ, "we are sanctified by the one offering of the body of Jesus Christ." This was Christ's sanctifying himself, in life and in death. This was what the Spirit of holiness worked in Him. This is what the same Spirit, the Spirit of life in Christ Jesus, will work in us: a life in the will of God is a life of holiness. Try to understand fully—Christ came to reveal what true holiness would be under the conditions of human life and weakness. He came to work it out for you that He might communicate it to you by His Spirit. Unless you intelligently understand and fully accept it, the Spirit cannot make you holy. With your whole heart try to take hold of this truth: the will of God unhesitatingly accepted is the power of holiness.

Any attempt to be holy as Christ is holy, with and in His

holiness, must start here. Many seek to take single parts of the life or image of Christ to imitate, and yet completely fail greatly in other points. They have not seen that the self-denial to which Jesus calls us really means the denial of self, in the full meaning of that word. In not one single thing is the will of self to be done: Jesus (who did the will of the Father only) must rule, not self. To "stand perfect and complete in all the will of God" must be the purpose, the prayer, the expectation of the disciple. Contrary to what we may fear, *it is possible to know the will of the Father in everything.* "If any man will do, he shall know." The Father will not keep the willing child in ignorance of His will. As the surrender to the Spirit of holiness, to Jesus and the dominion of His holy life, becomes more natural and complete, then sin and self-will will be discovered, the spiritual understanding will be increased and the law written in the inward parts become legible and intelligible. There need be no fear that it is not possible to do the will of the Father when it is known. When once the grief of failure and sin has driven the believer into the experience of Romans 7, and the "delight in the law of God after the inward man" has proved its earnestness in the cry, "O wretched man that I am"—then deliverance will come through Jesus Christ. The Spirit works not only to will but to do. Where the believer could only complain, "To perform that which is good, I find not," now the Spirit gives the strength to say, "The law of the Spirit of life in Christ Jesus hath made me free from the law of sin and death."

In this faith—that it is possible to know and do the will of God in all things—take over from Him, in whom alone you are holy, as your life principle: "I come to do thy will, O God." It is the principle of the resurrection life. Without it Jesus would never have been raised again. It is the principle of the new life in you. Accept it. Study it. Realize it. Act it out. Many a believer has found that a few simple words of dedication, expressive of the purpose to do God's will in everything, have been an entrance into the joy and power of the resurrection life previously unknown. The will of God is the complete expression of His moral perfection, His divine holiness. To take one's place in the center of that will, to live it out, to be borne and sustained by it—all these were the power of that life of Jesus that could not be held by death, that could not help but burst out in resurrection glory. What it was to Jesus it will be to us.

Holiness is life: this is the simplest expression of the truth our text teaches. There can be no holiness until there be a new life implanted. The new life cannot grow and break forth in resurrection power, cannot bring forth fruit except by growing in holiness. As long as the believer is living the mixed life, part in the flesh and part in the spirit, with some of self and some of Christ, he seeks in vain for holiness. It is the new life that is the holy life: the full apprehension of it in faith and the full surrender to it in conduct will be the highway of holiness. Jesus lived and died and rose again to prepare for us a new nature, to be received day by day in the obedience of faith. We "have put on the new man, which after God is created in righteousness and true holiness." Let the inner life, hidden with Christ in God, and also hidden deep within the recesses of our inmost being, be acknowledged, waited on, yielded to. It will work itself out in all the beauties of holiness.

Further, this life is not like the life of nature, a blind, nonconscious principle, involuntarily working toward its object in unresisting obedience to the law of its being. This life is the Spirit of life in Christ Jesus—the Spirit of holiness—the Holy Spirit dwelling in us as a divine person, entering into fellowship with us, and leading us into the fellowship of the living Christ. It is this that fills our life with hope and joy. The risen Savior breathed the Holy Spirit on His disciples: the Spirit brings the Risen One into the field, into our hearts, as a personal friend, as a living guide and strengthener. The Spirit of holiness is the Spirit, the presence, and the power of the living Christ. Jesus said of the Spirit, "Ye know him." Is not our great need to know this Holy Spirit, the Spirit of Christ, of His holiness and of ours? How can we "walk after the Spirit" and follow His leading if we do not know Him or His voice or His way?

One more lesson: It is out of the grave of the flesh and the will of self that the Spirit of holiness breaks out in resurrection power. We must accept death to the flesh and death to self with its willing and working as the birthplace of our experience of the power of the Spirit of holiness. In each struggle with sin, in each exercise of faith or prayer, we must enter into the death of Jesus and the death to self. Since "we are not sufficient to think anything as of ourselves," we must in quiet faith expect the Spirit of Christ to do His work. The Spirit will work, strengthening you mightily in the inner man and building up within you a holy temple for the Lord. And the time will come (if not yet, maybe soon) when the conscious indwelling of Christ in your heart by faith, the full revelation and enthronement of Him as ruler and keeper of heart and life, shall have become a personal experience. It is according to the Spirit of holiness, by the resurrection from the dead, that the Son of God will be declared with power in the kingdom that is within you.

Prayer

Most Holy Lord God, we do bless you that you raised your Son from the dead and gave Him glory that our faith and hope might be in you. You made His resurrection the power of eternal life in us, and now, just as He was raised, so we may walk in newness of life. As the Spirit of holiness dwelt and wrought in Him, it dwells and works in us and becomes in us the Spirit of life.

O God, we beseech you to perfect your work in your saints. Give them a deeper sense of the holy calling with which you have called them in Christ, the Risen One. Help all to accept the Spirit of His life on earth and delight in the will of God as the spirit of their life. May those who have never yet fully accepted this be brought to do it, and in faith of the power of the new life to say, I accept the will of God as my only law. May the Spirit of holiness be the spirit of their lives!

Father, we beseech you, let Christ thus, in ever-increasing experience of His resurrection power, be revealed in our hearts as the Son of God, Lord and ruler within us. Let His life within inspire all the outer life, so that in the home and society, in thought and speech and action, in religion and in business, His life may shine out from us in the beauty of holiness. Amen.

Personal Application

1. Scripture regards the resurrection in two different aspects. In one view, it is the title to the new life, the source

of our justification (Rom. 4:25; 1 Cor. 15:17). In another, it is our regeneration, the power of the new life working in us, the source of our sanctification (Rom. 6:4; 1 Pet. 1:3). Pardon and holiness are inseparable; they have the same source—union with the risen, living Christ.

2. The blessedness to the disciples of having a risen Christ was this: He, whom they thought dead, came and revealed himself to them. Christ lives to reveal himself to you and to me; wait on Him, trust Him for this. He will reveal himself to you as your sanctification. See to it that you have Him in living possession, and you have His holiness.

3. The life of Christ is the holiness of Christ. The reason we so often fail in the pursuit of holiness is that the old life, the flesh, in its own strength seeks for holiness as a beautiful garment to wear and enter heaven with. It is the daily death to self out of which the life of Christ rises up.

4. To die thus, to live thus in Christ, to be holy—how can we attain it? It all comes "according to the Spirit of holiness." Have the Holy Spirit within you. Say daily, "I believe in the Holy Spirit."

5. Holy in Christ. When Christ lives in us, and His mind (as it found expression in His words and work on earth) enters and fills our will and personal consciousness, then our union with Him becomes what He meant it to be. It is the Spirit of His holy conduct, the Spirit of His sanctity, that must be in us.

CHAPTER TWENTY

Holiness and Liberty

"Being then made free from sin, ye became the servants of righteousness. . . . Now yield your members servants to righteousness unto holiness. Now being made free from sin, and become servants to God, ye have your fruit unto holiness, and the end everlasting life" (Rom. 6:18, 19, 22).

"Our liberty which we have in Christ Jesus" (Gal. 2:4).

"Stand fast therefore in the liberty wherewith Christ hath made us free, and be not entangled again with the yoke of bondage" (Gal. 5:1).

No possession is more precious or priceless than liberty. Nothing is more inspiring and elevating. On the other hand, nothing is more depressing and degrading than slavery. It robs a man of what constitutes his manhood, the power of self-decision, self-action, of being and doing what he would.

Sin is slavery—the bondage to a foreign power that has obtained control over us, and often compels a most reluctant service. The redemption of Christ restores our liberty and sets us free from the power of sin. If we are truly to live as redeemed ones, we need not only to look at the work Christ did to accomplish our redemption, but to accept and comprehend how complete, how sure, how absolute the liberty is with which He has made us free. It is only as we "stand fast in our liberty in Christ Jesus" that we can have our fruit unto sanctification.

It is remarkable how seldom the word holy occurs in the

great argument of Romans and how, where twice used in chapter 6 in the expression "unto sanctification," it is distinctly set forth as the aim and fruit to be reached through a life of righteousness. The twice repeated "unto sanctification," pointing to a result to be obtained, is preceded by a twice-repeated "being made free from sin and become servants of righteousness." It teaches us how the liberty from the power of sin and the surrender to the service of righteousness are not yet of themselves holiness, but they are the sure and only path by which it can be reached. A true insight and a full entering into our freedom from sin in Christ are indispensable to a life of holiness. It was when Israel was freed from Pharaoh that God began to reveal himself as the Holy One; it is as we know ourselves "freed from sin," delivered from the hand of all our enemies, that we shall serve God in righteousness and holiness all the days of our life.

"Being made free from sin": to understand this correctly, we must beware of a twofold error. Neither narrow it down to less nor put more into it than the Holy Spirit means here. Paul is speaking neither of an imputation nor an experience. We must not limit the meaning to freeing from the curse or punishment of sin. The context shows that he is speaking, not of our judicial standing, but of a spiritual reality—our being in living union with Christ in His death and resurrection, and so being completely removed from the dominion or power of sin. "Sin shall not have dominion over you." Neither is he as yet speaking of an experience where we feel that we are free from all sin. He speaks of the great objective fact of Christ's having finally delivered us from the power which sin had, to compel us to do its will and its works. He urges us, in the faith of this glorious fact, boldly to refuse to listen to the bidding or temptation to sin. To know our liberty which we have in Christ, our freedom from sin's mastery and power, is the way to realize it as an experience.

In olden times, when Turks or Moors often made slaves of Christians, large sums were frequently paid to ransom those who were in bondage. But it happened more than once that the ransomed ones, far in the interior of the slave country, never received the news; the masters were only too glad to keep it from them. Others received the word, but had grown too accustomed to their bondage to rouse themselves for the effort of reaching the coast. Slothfulness or hopelessness kept them in slavery. They could not believe that they would ever be able to reach the land of liberty in safety. The ransom had been paid. In truth they were free; but by reason of ignorance or want of courage, in actuality they remained in bondage. Christ's redemption has so completely made an end of sin and the legal power it had over us—for "the strength of sin is the law"—that in the deepest reality, sin has no power to compel our obedience. Only as we allow it to reign again and yield ourselves again as its servants can it exercise dominion over us. Satan does his utmost to keep believers in ignorance of this completeness of their freedom from his slavery. Believers are limited in their own thoughts of what redemption means, and weak in their desire and prayers to see and possess its fullness of deliverance and blessing. Because of this the experience of the extent to which the freedom from sin can be realized is so feeble compared to all that is available. "Where the Spirit of the Lord is, there is liberty." By the Holy Spirit with His light and leading within, humbly watched for and yielded to, this liberty becomes our possession.

In the sixth chapter of Romans Paul speaks of freedom from sin and in chapter seven (vv. 3, 4, 6) of freedom from the law, as both privileges being ours in Christ and in union with Him. In chapter eight (v. 2) he speaks of this freedom as having become ours in experience. He says, "The law of the Spirit of life in Christ Jesus hath made me free from the law of sin and death." The freedom which is ours in Christ must become ours in personal appropriation and enjoyment through the Holy Spirit. The latter depends on the former: the fuller the faith, the clearer the insight, the more triumphant the glorying in Christ Jesus and the liberty with which He has made us free, the speedier and the fuller the entrance into the glorious liberty of the children of God. Just as the liberty is in Christ alone, so the Spirit of Christ alone makes it ours in practical possession and keeps us dwelling in it. "The spirit of the life in Christ Jesus hath made me free from the law of sin and death." "Where the Spirit of the Lord is, there is liberty." The Spirit reveals Jesus to us as Lord and Master, the new Master, who alone has authority over us. He leads us to yield ourselves, to present our members, to surrender our whole life to the service of God in Christ. As He does this, our faith in the freedom from sin becomes a consciousness and a realization. Believing in the completeness of the redemption, the captive goes forth as "the Lord's freedman." He knows now that sin no longer has power for one moment to command obedience. It may seek to assert its old right; it may speak in the tone of authority; it may frighten into fear and submission; but it has no power over us, unless we, forgetting our freedom, yield to its temptation and give it power.

We are the Lord's freedmen. "We have our liberty in Christ Jesus." In Romans seven Paul describes the terrible struggles of the soul who still seeks to fulfill the law but finds itself utterly helpless—sold under sin, a captive and a slave, without the liberty to do what the whole heart desires. But when the Spirit takes the place of the law, the complaint "O wretched man that I am" is changed into the song of victory, "I thank God, through Jesus Christ, the law of the Spirit of life hath made me free."

What numberless complaints of insufficient strength to do God's will, of unsuccessful effort and disappointed hopes and continual failure re-echo in a thousand different forms the complaint of the captive, "O wretched man that I am!" Thank God! there is deliverance. "With freedom did Christ set us free! Stand fast therefore, and be not entangled again in a yoke of bondage." Satan is always trying to lay on us again either the yoke of sin or the law, and to create again the spirit of bondage, as if sin or the law with their demands somehow had power over us. Do not let him ensnare you with these tricks. Stand fast in the liberty with which Christ has made you free. Listen to the message: "Being made free from sin, ye became servants unto righteousness; now yield your members servants to righteousness unto sanctification." "Having been made free from sin, and having been enslaved unto God, ye have your fruit unto sanctification." To be holy, you must be free, perfectly free—free for Jesus to rule you and lead you; free for the Holy Spirit to work through you, to breathe in you, to work His secret, gentle, but mighty work, so that you may mature into all this liberty Jesus has won for you. The temple could not be sanctified by the indwelling of God unless it was free from every other master and every other use, to be for God and His service alone. The inner temple of our heart cannot be truly and fully sanctified unless we are free from every other master and power, from every yoke of bondage or fear or doubt, free to let His Spirit lead us into the perfect liberty which has its fruit in true holiness.

Being made free from sin, having become servants of righteousness, you have your fruit of holiness, and the end is life everlasting. Freedom, righteousness, holiness—these are steps on the way to the coming glory. The more deeply we enter by faith into our liberty which we have in Christ, the more joyfully and confidently we present our members to God as instruments of righteousness. The God is the Father whose will we delight to do, whose service is perfect liberty. The Redeemer is the Master, to whom love binds us in willing obedience. The liberty is not lawlessness: "We are delivered from our enemies, that we may serve him in righteousness and holiness all the days of our life."

The liberty is the condition of the righteousness; and this again of the holiness. The doing of God's will leads to that fellowship, that heart sympathy with God himself, out of which comes that reflection of the divine presence, which is holiness. Being made free from sin, being made the slaves of righteousness and of God, we have our fruit unto holiness, and the end—the fruit of holiness, when ripe, becomes the seed of—everlasting life.

Prayer

Most glorious God, I pray to you to open my eyes to this wonderful liberty with which Christ has made me free. May I enter fully into your word, that sin shall have no dominion over me because I am not under the law but under grace. May I know my liberty which I have in Christ Jesus, and stand fast in it.

Father, your service is perfect liberty: reveal this too to me. You are the infinitely free, and your will knows no limits except what its own perfection has placed. And you invite us into your will that we may be free as you are. O my God, show me the beauty of your will that can free me from self and from sin, and let it be my only blessedness. Let the service of righ-

*teousness so be a joy and a strength to me, having its fruit
unto sanctification, leading me into your holiness.*

*Blessed Lord Jesus! my deliverer and my liberty, I belong
to you. I give myself to your will, to know no will but yours.
Master! you and you alone would I serve. I have my liberty in
you, be my keeper. I cannot stand for one moment without
you. In you I can stand fast: in you I put my trust.*

*Most Holy God, as your free, obedient, loving child, you
will make me holy. Amen.*

Personal Application

1. Liberty is the power to carry out unhindered the impulse of our nature. In Christ the child of God is free from
every power that could hinder his acting out the law of his
new nature.

2. This liberty is of faith (Gal. 5:5, 6). By faith in Christ
I enter into this liberty and stand in it.

3. This liberty is of the Holy Spirit. "Where the Spirit of
the Lord is, there is liberty." "If ye be led of the Spirit, ye
are not under the law." A heart filled with the Spirit is made
free indeed. But we are not made free that we may do our
own will. No, made free to follow the leading of the Holy
Spirit. "Where the Spirit is, there is liberty."

4. This liberty is in love. "Ye were called for freedom;
only use not your freedom for an occasion to the flesh, but
through love be servants one to another." The freedom with
which the Son makes free is a freedom to become like Him,
to love and to serve. "Though I was free from all men, I
brought myself under bondage to all, that I might gain the
more." This is the liberty of love.

5. "Being made free from sin, ye became servants of righteousness unto sanctification." "Let my people go, that they
may serve me." It is only the man who lives righteously that
can become holy.

6. This liberty is a thing of joy and singing.

7. This liberty is the groundwork of holiness. The Redeemer who makes free is God the Holy One. As the Holy
Spirit He leads into the full possession of it. To be so free
from everything that God can take complete possession is to
be holy.

CHAPTER TWENTY-ONE

Holiness and Happiness

"For the kingdom of God is . . . joy in the Holy Ghost" (Rom. 14:17).
"The disciples were filled with joy and with the Holy Ghost" (Acts 13:52).

"And Nehemiah . . . said . . . This day is holy unto the Lord your God; mourn not, nor weep . . . for the joy of the Lord is your strength. So the Levites stilled all the people, saying, Hold your peace, for the day is holy; neither be ye grieved. And all the people went their way . . . to make great mirth, because they had understood the words" (Neh. 8:9–12).

The deep significance of joy in the Christian life is hardly understood. Too often it is regarded as something secondary, whereas its presence is essential as the proof that God does indeed satisfy us, and that His service is our delight. In our home life we do not feel satisfied if only the bare standards of conduct are observed, and each only does his duty to the other; true love makes us happy in each other. As love gives out its warmth of affection, gladness is the sunshine that fills the home with its brightness. Even in suffering or poverty, the members of a loving family are a joy to each other. Without this gladness, especially, there is no true obedience on the part of the children. It is not the mere fulfillment of a command or performance of a service that a parent looks for—it is the willing, joyful alacrity with which it is done that makes it pleasing.

It is the same in the relationship of God's children with their Father. Even in our effort to live a life of consecration and gospel obedience, we are continually in danger of coming under the

139

law again, with its, *"Thou shalt."* The consequence always is failure. The law only works wrath; it gives neither life nor strength. Only as long as we are standing in the joy of our deliverance from sin, in the joy of our Lord and His love and what He is for us, the joy of His presence, will we have the power to serve and obey. It is only when made free from every master, from sin and self and the law, and only when rejoicing in this liberty, that we have the power to render service that is satisfying either to God or to ourselves. "I will see you again," Jesus said, "and your heart shall rejoice, and your joy shall no man take from you." Joy is the evidence and the condition of the abiding personal presence of Jesus.

If holiness be the beauty and the glory of the life of faith, then it is manifest that here especially the element of joy should not be missing. We have already seen how the first mention of God as the Holy One was in the song of praise on the shore of the Red Sea; how Hannah and Mary in their moments of inspiration praised God as the Holy One; how the name of the Thrice Holy in heaven comes to us in the song of the seraphs; and how before the throne both the living creatures and the conquering multitude who sing the song of the Lamb, adore God as the Holy One. We are to "worship him in the beauty of holiness," and "to sing praise at the remembrance of his holiness." It is only in the spirit of worship and praise and joy that we fully can know God as holy. Much more, only under the inspiration of adoring love and joy can we ourselves be made holy. As we cease from all fear and anxiety, from all strain and effort, and rest with singing in what Jesus is in His finished work as our sanctification, as we rest and rejoice in Him, we shall be made partakers of His holiness. It is the day of rest, the day that God has blessed, the day of blessing and gladness, and it is the day He blessed that is His holy day. Holiness and blessedness are inseparable.

But is not this contrary to the teaching of Scripture and the experience of the saints? Are not suffering and sorrow among God's chosen means of sanctification? Are not the promises made to the broken in heart, the poor in spirit, and the mourner? Are not self-denial and the forsaking of all we have, the crucifixion with Christ and the dying daily, the path to holiness? And is not all this more matter of sorrow and pain than of joy and gladness?

The answer will be found in the right understanding of the

life of faith. Faith lifts above, and gives possession of, what is the very opposite of what we feel or experience. In the Christian life there is always a paradox: things which appear irreconcilable opposites are found side by side at the same moment. Paul expresses it in the words, "As dying, and, behold, we live; as sorrowful, yet always rejoicing; as poor, yet making many rich; as having nothing, yet possessing all things." And elsewhere thus, "When I am weak, then am I strong." The apparent contradiction has its reconciliation, not only in the union of the two lives—the human and the divine—in the person of each believer, but especially in our being, simultaneously, partakers of the death and the resurrection of Christ. Christ's death was one of pain and suffering, a real and terrible death, a rending asunder of the bonds that united soul and body, spirit and flesh. The power of that death works in us. We must let it work mightily if we are to live holy lives, for in that death He sanctified himself that we ourselves might be sanctified in truth. Like His, our holiness is in the death to our own will and to all our own life.

But—this we must seek to grasp—we do not approach death from the side from which Christ met it, as an enemy to be conquered, as a suffering to be borne, before the new life can be entered on. No, the believer who knows what Christ is as the Risen One approaches death, the crucifixion of self and the flesh and the world, from the resurrection side, the place of victory, in the power of the living Christ. When we were baptized into Christ, we were baptized into His death and resurrection as ours, and Christ himself, the risen, living Lord, leads us triumphantly into the experience of the power of His death. To the believer who truly lives by faith and does not try by his own struggles to crucify and mortify the flesh, but knows the living Lord, the deep resurrection joy never for a moment forsakes Him. Instead, that joy is his strength for what may appear to others to be only painful sacrifice and cross-bearing. He says with Paul, "I glory in the cross through which I have been crucified." He never, as so many do, asks Paul's question, "Who shall deliver me from the body of this death?" without giving the joyful and triumphant answer as a present experience, "I thank God, through Jesus Christ our Lord," and "Thanks be to God, which always leadeth us in triumph in Christ." It is only the joy of a present Savior—the experience of a perfect salvation, and the joy of a resurrection life—which gives the power to enter deeply and fully into the death that Christ died, and to yield our will and our life to be wholly sanctified to God. In the joy of that life from which the power of the death is never absent, it is possible to say with the Apostle each moment, "As dying, and, behold, we live; as sorrowful, yet always rejoicing."

Let us seek to learn the two lessons: Holiness is essential to true happiness; happiness is essential to true holiness.

Holiness is essential to true happiness. If you would have joy, the fullness of joy, an abiding joy which nothing can take away, be holy as God is holy. Holiness is blessedness. Nothing but sin can darken or interrupt our joy. Whatever be our trial or temptation, the joy of Jesus of which Peter says, "In whom ye now rejoice with joy unspeakable," can more than compensate and outweigh. If we lose our joy, it must be because of sin. It may be an actual transgression or an unconscious following of self or the world. It may be the stain on our conscience of something doubtful. Or perhaps it might be unbelief that wants to live by sight, and thinks more of itself and its joy than of the Lord alone. Whatever it be, remember that nothing can take away our joy except sin. If we would live lives of joy, assuring God and man and ourselves that our Lord is more than anything or everything to us, then be holy! Glory in Him who is our holiness; in His presence is fullness of joy. Live in the Kingdom, which is joy in the Holy Spirit. The Spirit of holiness is the Spirit of joy, because He is the Spirit of God. The saints, God's holy ones, are those who will shout for joy.

Happiness is essential to true holiness. If you want to be a holy Christian, you must be a happy Christian. Jesus was anointed by God with "the oil of gladness" that He might give us "the oil of joy." In all our efforts after holiness, the wheels will move heavily if there is no oil of joy; this alone removes all strain and friction, and makes the onward progress easy and delightful. Study to understand the divine value of joy. It is the evidence of your being in the Father's presence and dwelling in His love. Joy is the proof of your being consciously free from the law and the strain of the spirit of bondage. Joy is the token of your freedom from care and responsibility, because you are rejoicing in Christ Jesus as your sanctification, your keeper and your strength. The secret of spiritual health and strength is joy, filling all your service with the happy, childlike assurance that the Father asks nothing for which He does not give strength, and that He accepts all that is done—however feebly—in this spirit. True happiness is always self-forgetful; it loses itself in the object of its joy. As the joy of the Holy Spirit fills us and we rejoice in God the Holy one through our Lord Jesus Christ, as we lose ourselves in the adoration and worship of the Thrice Holy, we become holy. Even here in the wilderness this is "the highway of holiness: the ransomed of the Lord shall come with singing; the redeemed shall walk there; everlasting joy shall be upon their heads; they shall obtain joy and gladness."

Do God's children understand that holiness is just another name—the true name—that God gives to happiness? To know that God does make us holy, that our holiness is in Christ and that Christ's Holy Spirit is within us is blessedness beyond description. Nothing is so attractive as joy. Do believers understand that this is the joy of the Lord—to be holy? Or is it not true that the idea of strain, sacrifice and sighing, of difficulty and distance so prevail that the thought of being holy hardly ever makes the heart glad? If this has been true, let it be so no longer. "Thou shalt glory in the Holy One of Israel." Let us claim this promise. Believe that our loving Father, our beloved Lord Jesus, and the Holy Spirit, who in dovelike gentleness rests within us, have undertaken the work, and are doing it. Let that assurance fill us with gladness. What we see in ourselves of holiness is not where we must look for joy—let us rejoice in the holiness of God in Christ as ours, let us rejoice in the Holy One of Israel. So shall our joy be unspeakable and unceasing; so shall we give Him the glory.

Prayer

Most Blessed God, I beg you to reveal to me and to all your children the secret of rejoicing in you, the Holy One of Israel.

You see how much of the service of your own dear children is still in the spirit of bondage, and how many have never yet believed that the highway of holiness is one on which they may walk with singing, and where they shall obtain joy and gladness. O Father, teach your children to rejoice in you.

Teach us that, in deep poverty of spirit, in humility and contrition and utter emptiness, in the consciousness that there is no holiness in us, we can sing all the day of your holiness as ours, of your glory which you lay upon us, and yet which all the time

*is yours alone. O Father, open wide to your children the blessed
mystery of the Kingdom, that faith which sees all in Christ and
nothing in itself; which indeed has and rejoices in all in Him;
which never has or rejoices in anything of self.*

*Blessed God, in your Word you have said, "The meek shall
increase their joy in the Lord, and the poor among men shall
rejoice in the Holy One of Israel." Help us, by your Holy Spirit,
in meekness and poverty of spirit, to live so in Christ that His
holiness may be our ever-increasing joy, and that in yourself, the
Holy One of Israel, we may rejoice always. May all see in us what
blessedness it is to live as God's holy ones. Amen.*

Personal Application

1. The great hindrance to joy in God is expecting to find
something in ourselves to rejoice over. At the beginning of this
pursuit of holiness we always expect to see a great change
wrought in ourselves. As we are led deeper and see what faith
and the faith-life are, we understand that although we do not
see the change we expected, still we may rejoice with joy unspeakable in what Jesus is. This is the secret of holiness.

2. Joy must be cultivated. To rejoice is a command more
frequently given than we may realize. It is part of the obedience
of faith, to rejoice when we do not feel like doing so. Faith rejoices and sings, because God is holy.

3. "Filled with joy and the Holy Ghost," "The kingdom is
joy in the Holy Ghost." The Holy Spirit, the Blessed Spirit of
Jesus, is within you, a very fountain of living water, of joy and
gladness. Seek to know Him, who dwells in you, to work all that
Jesus has for you. He will be in you the Spirit of faith and of
joy.

4. Love and joy ever keep company. Love, denying and forgetting itself for the brethren and the lost, living in them, finds
the joy of God. "The kingdom of God is joy in the Holy Ghost."

CHAPTER TWENTY-TWO

In Christ Our Sanctification

"But of [God] are ye in Christ Jesus, who of God is made unto us wisdom, and righteousness, and sanctification and redemption: that, according as it is written, He that glorieth, let him glory in the Lord" (1 Cor. 1:30, 31).

These words lead us to the very center of God's revelation of the way of holiness. We know the steps of the road which lead here. He is holy and holiness is His. He makes holy by coming near. His presence is holiness. In Christ's life, the holiness that before had only been revealed in symbol and as a promise of good things to come, now really took possession of a human will and was made one with true human nature. In His death every obstacle was removed that could prevent the transmission of that holy nature to us: Christ truly became our sanctification. In the Holy Spirit the actual communication of that holiness took place. And now we want to understand what the work is that the Holy Spirit does, and how He communicates this holy nature to us. We want to know what our relation is to Christ as our sanctification, and what position we have to take toward Him, that in its fullness and its power it may do its work for us.

The divine answer to this question is, "Of God are ye in Christ." We need to understand what our position is and what this life in Christ is, and how on our part they may be accepted and maintained. Of this we may be sure, that this is not something high and beyond our reach. There need be no exhausting effort or hopeless sighing, "Who shall ascend into heaven, that is, to bring Christ down from above?" This life is meant for the sinful and the weary, for the unworthy and the impotent. It is a life that is the gift of the Father's love and a life that He himself will reveal in each one who comes in childlike trust to Him. It is a life that is meant for our everyday life. In every varying circumstance and situation this life will make and keep us holy.

"Of God are ye in Christ." Before our Blessed Lord left the world, He said, "Lo! I am with you alway, even to the end of the world." And it is written of Him: "He that descended is the same that ascended far above all the heavens, that he might fill all things." "The church is his body, the fulness of him that filleth all in all." In the Holy Spirit the Lord Jesus is with His people here on earth. Though unseen and not in the flesh, His personal presence is as real on earth as when He walked with His disciples. In regeneration the believer is taken out of his old place "in the flesh." He is no longer in the flesh, but in the spirit (Rom. 8:9). He is really and actually in Christ. The living Christ is around him by His holy presence. Wherever and whatever he be, however ignorant of his position or however unfaithful to it, he is in Christ. By an act of divine and omnipotent grace, he has been planted into Christ, encircled on every side by the power and the love of Him who fills all things, whose fullness especially dwells in His body here below, the Church.

How can one who longs to know Christ fully as his sanctification live out what God means and has provided in this— "in Christ"? The first thing to remember is that it is a thing of faith and not of feeling. The promise of the indwelling and the quickening of the Holy One is to the humble and contrite. Just when I feel most deeply that I am not holy and can do nothing to make myself holy, when I feel ashamed of myself, that is the time to turn from self and very quietly to say: "I am in Christ. Here He is all around me. Like the air that surrounds me, like the light that shines on me, here is my Lord Jesus with me in His hidden but divine and most real presence. My faith must in quiet rest and trust bow before the Father, of whom and by whose mighty grace I am in Christ." He will reveal this to me with ever-growing clearness and power. He does it as I believe, and in believing I open my whole soul to receive what is implied in it: the sense of sinfulness and unholiness must become the strength of my trust and dependence. In such faith I abide in Christ.

But because it is of faith, therefore it is of the Holy Spirit. Of God are ye in Christ. It is not as if God placed and planted us in Christ, and left it to us now to maintain the union. No. God is the Eternal One, the God of the everlasting life, who works every moment in a power that does not for one moment cease. What God gives, He continues with a never-ceasing giving. It is He who by the Holy Spirit makes this life in Christ a blessed reality in our consciousness. "We have received the Spirit of God that we might know the things that are freely given us of God." Faith is not only dependent on God for the gift it is to accept but also for the power to accept. Faith not only needs the Son as its filling and its food, it needs the Spirit as its power to receive and hold. And so the blessed possession of all that it means to be in Christ our sanctification comes as we learn to bow before God in believing prayer for the mighty workings of the Spirit, and in deep childlike trust that He will reveal and glorify in us this Christ our sanctification in whom we are.

How will the Spirit reveal this Christ in whom we are? It will be especially as the Living One, the personal friend and master. Christ is not only our example and our ideal. His life is not only an atmosphere and an inspiration, such as we might say about a man who mightily influences us by his writings. Christ is not only a treasury and a fullness of grace and power into which the Spirit is to lead us, but Christ is the living Savior, with a heart that beats with a love that is most tenderly human and yet divine. In this love He comes near and receives us into this love when the Father plants us into Him. In the power of a personal love, He wishes to exercise influence and unite us with himself. In that love of His we have the guarantee that His holiness will enter us, in that love the great power by which it enters. As the Spirit reveals to us where we are dwelling—in Christ and His love— and that this Christ is a living Lord and Savior, there wakens within us the enthusiasm of a personal attachment and the devotion of a loving allegiance that make us wholly His. Seeing this, it becomes possible for us to believe that we can be holy. We feel sure that in the path of holiness we can go from strength to strength.

Such believing insight into our relation to Christ as being in Him, and such personal attachment to Him who has received us into His love and keeps us abiding there, becomes the source of a new obedience. The will of God comes to us in the light of Christ's life and His love—each command first fulfilled by Him, and then passed on to us as the sure and blessed help to more perfect fellowship with the Father and His holiness. In the power of the Holy Spirit, Christ becomes Lord and King in the soul, guiding the will into all the perfect will of God, and proving himself to be its sanctification, as He crowns its obedience with ever larger inflow of the presence and the holiness of God.

Are you discouraged as you think of the holy life you shall live? Take courage. Could God have devised anything more wonderful or beautiful than He has for such sinful, impotent creatures? Imagine, Christ—God's own Son—made to be sanctification to you. The mighty, loving, holy Christ was sanctified through suffering so that He might have sympathy with you, and was given to make you holy. Could you possibly desire more? Yes, because He has given even more: "Of God you are in him." Whether you understand it or not, however feebly you realize it, the fact is divinely true and real. You are in Christ, by an act of God's own mighty power. And God himself longs to establish and confirm you there, in Christ, to the end. Greatest wonder of all, you have the Holy Spirit within you to teach you to know and believe and receive all that there is in Christ for you. And if you will only confess that there is in you no wisdom or power for holiness, none at all, and allow Christ, "the Wisdom of God and the Power of God," to lead you on by the Holy Spirit within you, and prove how completely, how faithfully, how mightily, He can be your sanctification. He will do it most gloriously.

Come and yield more fully to God's way of holiness. Let Christ be your sanctification. Not a distant Christ to whom you look but a Christ very near, all around you, in whom you are. Not a Christ after the flesh, a Christ of the past, but a present Christ in the power of the Holy Spirit. Not a Christ whom you can know by your wisdom, but the Christ of God who is a Spirit, and whom the Spirit within you, as you die to the flesh and self, will reveal in power. Not a limited Christ such as your finite mind might conceive but a Christ according to the greatness of the heart and love of God. Come and accept this Christ and rejoice in Him! Be content to leave all your weakness, foolishness and faithlessness to Him in the quiet confidence that He will do for you more than you can think. And so from now on let it be as written, He that glorieth, let him glory in the Lord.

Prayer

Most Blessed Father, I bow in speechless adoration before the holy mystery of your divine love. . . .

Oh, forgive me, that I have known and believed it so much less than it deserves to be known and believed.

Accept my praise for what I have seen and tasted of its divine blessedness. Accept, Lord God, the praise of a glad and loving heart that only knows that it never can praise you enough.

Hear my prayer, O my Father, that in the power of your Holy Spirit who dwells in me, I may each day accept and live out fully what you have given me in Christ my sanctification. May the unsearchable riches there are in Him be the daily supply for my every need. May His holiness, His delight in your will, indeed become mine. Teach me, above all, how this can most surely be, because I am, through the work of your almighty quickening power in Him, kept there by you. My Father, my faith cries out: "I can be holy, blessed be my Lord Jesus!"

In this faith I yield myself to you, Lord Jesus, my King and Master, to do your will alone. In everything I do, great or small, I would act as one sanctified in Jesus, united to God's will in Him. You alone can teach me to do this, can give me strength to perform it. But I trust in you—are you not Christ my sanctification? Blessed Lord! I do trust you. Amen.

Personal Application

1. Christ, as He lived and died on earth, is our sanctification. His life, the Spirit of His life, is what constitutes our

holiness. To be in perfect harmony with Christ, to have His mind, is to be holy.

2. Christ's holiness had two sides. God sanctified Him by His Spirit; Christ sanctified himself by following the leading of the Spirit, by giving up His will to God in everything. So God has made us holy in Christ; and so we follow after and perfect holiness by yielding ourselves to God's Spirit, by giving up our will and living in the will of God.

3. We would do well to take in every aspect of what God has revealed of holiness in His Word. But let us never weary ourselves by seeking to grasp all completely. Let us return to the simplicity that is in Jesus. To bow at His feet, to believe that He knows all we need and has it all—and loves to give it all—is rest. Holiness is resting in Jesus the rest of God. Let all our thoughts be joined in this one: Jesus, Blessed Jesus.

4. This holy life in Christ is for today as you read. For today He is made of God unto you sanctification. Today He will indeed be your holiness. Believe in Him for it, trust Him, praise Him. And remember: you are in Him.

CHAPTER TWENTY-THREE

Holiness and the Body

*"The temple of God is holy, which temple ye are. The body is . . .
for the Lord; and the Lord for the body. . . . Know ye not that your
body is the temple of the Holy Ghost which is in you . . . therefore
glorify God in your body"* (1 Cor. 3:17; 6:13, 19, 20).

*"The unmarried woman careth for the things of the Lord, that
she may be holy both in body and in spirit"* (1 Cor. 7:34).

"Present your bodies a living sacrifice, holy, acceptable unto God"
(Rom. 12:1).

Coming into the world, our Blessed Lord said, "A body
didst though prepare for me; lo, I come to do thy will, O God."
Leaving this world again, it was in His own body that He
bore our sins upon the tree. So it was in the body, no less
than in soul and spirit, that He did the will of God. And
therefore it is said, "By which will we have been sanctified
through the offering of the body of Jesus Christ once for all."

When praying for the Thessalonians and their sanctification, Paul says, "And the God of peace himself sanctify you
wholly; and may your spirit and soul and body be preserved
entire, without blame, at the coming of our Lord Jesus Christ."
Of himself he had spoken as "always bearing about in the
body the dying of Jesus, that the life also of Jesus may be
manifested in our body. For we which live are always delivered unto death for Jesus' sake, that the life also of Jesus
may be manifested in our mortal flesh." His earnest expectation and hope was "that Christ be magnified in my body,

whether by life or by death." The relation between body and spirit is so intimate, the power of sin in the spirit comes so much through the body, and the body is so distinctly the object both of Christ's redemption and the Holy Spirit's renewal, that our study of holiness will be seriously defective if we do not take in the teaching of Scripture on holiness in the body.

A good comparison is that the body is to the soul and spirit dwelling and acting within it like the walls of the city. Through them the enemy enters in. In time of war, the defense of the walls is of prime importance. Often, because the believer does not know the importance of keeping the walls defended by keeping the body sanctified, he fails to keep the soul and spirit preserved blameless. Or perhaps he does not understand that the guarding and sanctifying of the body in all its parts must be a distinct work of faith. It must be accomplished directly through the mighty power of Jesus and the indwelling of the Spirit, just as is the renewing of the inner life. Is it because he does not know this that progress is so feeble? The rule of the city we entrust to Jesus, but the defense of the walls we keep in our own hands. The King does not keep us as we expected and we cannot discover the secret of failure. It is the God of peace himself who sanctifies wholly, who must preserve spirit and soul and body complete and without blame. The tabernacle with its wood, the temple with its stone, were as holy as all that was included within their walls. God's holy ones need the body to be holy.

To fully understand this, let us remember it was through the body that sin entered. "The woman saw that the tree was good for food"; this was the temptation in the flesh. Through this the soul was reached. "It was a delight to the eyes." Through the soul it then passed into the spirit, "And to be desired to make one wise." In John's description of what is in the world (1 John 2:16), we find the same threefold division, "the lust of the flesh, the lust of the eyes, and the pride of life." The three temptations of Jesus by Satan correspond exactly: he first sought to reach Him through the body, suggesting he satisfy His hunger by making bread; the second (see Luke 4) appealed to the soul, in the vision of the kingdoms of this world and their glory; the third to the spirit, in the call to assert and prove His divine sonship by casting himself down. Even to the Son of God the first temptation came, just as to Adam and all in the world, as lust of the flesh, the desire to gratify the natural and lawful appetite of hunger. We cannot stress too much that it was on a question of eating what appeared good for food that man's first sin was committed, and that that same question of eating to satisfy hunger was the battleground on which the Redeemer's first encounter with Satan took place. Many Christians are unknowingly foiled by Satan on the question of eating and drinking what is good and lawful. To have every appetite of the body under the rule and regulation of the Holy Spirit appears to some needless, to others too difficult. And yet it must be, if the body is to be holy, as God's temple, and we are to glorify Him in our body and our spirit. The first attacks of sin are made through the body; in the body the complete victory will be gained.

What Scripture teaches about the intimacy of connection between the body and spirit, physiology confirms. Things that appear at first to be merely physical transgressions leave a stain and have a degrading influence on the soul, and through it drag down the spirit. On the other hand, spiritual sins—sins of thought and imagination and disposition—pass through the soul into the body, fix themselves in the nervous constitution, and express themselves even in the countenance and the habits or tendencies of the body. If we are to perfect holiness, we must cleanse ourselves from all defilement of flesh *and* spirit, not only in the region of the spirit. "If through the Spirit ye do make dead the deeds of the body, ye shall live." If we are indeed to be cleansed from sin and made holy unto God, the body as the outer defense must especially be well protected from the power of Satan and of sin.

How is this to be done? God has made very special provision for this. Holy Scripture speaks explicitly of the Holy Spirit, the Spirit that communicates holiness, in connection with the body. At first sight it looks as if the expression *your bodies* were simply used as equivalent to *your persons, your selves*. But as insight deepens into the power of sin in the body, and the need of a special deliverance there quickens our perception, we see what is meant by the body being the temple of the Holy Spirit. We notice that it is particularly sins of the body that Paul says defile God's holy temple, and how it is through the power of the Holy Spirit in the body that he would have us glorify God. "Know ye not that your body is the temple of the Holy Ghost: glorify God therefore, in the power of the Holy Spirit, in your body." The Holy Spirit must not only exercise a restraining and regulating influence on the appetites of the body and their gratification so that they be in moderation and temperance—this is only the negative side—but there must be a positive spiritual element, making the exercise of natural functions a service of holy joy and liberty to the glory of God. No longer need they be a threatened hindrance to the life of obedience and fellowship, but instead a means of grace, a real help to the spiritual life. Only in a body that is full of the holy life, totally possessed by God's Spirit, will this be the case.

And how can this change be accomplished? In the true Christian life, self-denial is the path to enjoyment, as are renunciation to possession and death to life. As long as there is anything that we think we have liberty and power to use or enjoy in the right way—if we only do so in moderation—we have not yet seen or confessed our own unholiness or the need of total renewal by the Holy Spirit. It is not enough to say, "Every creature of God is good, if it be received with thanksgiving"; we must remember the addition, "for it is sanctified by the word and by prayer." This sanctifying of every creature and its use is a thing as real and solemn as the sanctifying of ourselves. And this will only be where, if need be, we sacrifice the gift and the liberty to use it, until God gives us the power to use it truly to His glory alone. Of one of the most sacred of divine institutions—marriage— Paul, who so denounces those who would forbid to marry, says distinctly that there may be cases in which a voluntary celibacy may be the surest and acceptable way of being "holy both in body and spirit." When to be holy as God is holy indeed becomes the overwhelming desire and aim of life, everything will either be cherished or surrendered, according to whether it promotes that supreme purpose. The actual and active presence of the Holy Spirit in the life of the body will be the fire that is kept burning continually on the altar.

How is this to be attained? With the body just as it is with the spirit, it is God who works; God in Christ is our keeper and our sanctifier. The guarding of the walls of the city must be entrusted to Him who rules within. "I am persuaded that He is able to guard my deposit," to keep that which I have committed to Him. This must become as definitely true of the body and of each of its functions that have caused doubt or stumbling, as it has been true of the soul we entrusted to Him for salvation. A fixed deposit in a bank is money given away out of my hands for safekeeping. Likewise the body or any part of it that needs to be made holy must be a deposit with Jesus. Faith must trust His acceptance and guarding of it; prayer and praise must daily renew the assurance, confirm the committal of the deposit and maintain the fellowship with Jesus. Abiding thus in Him and His holiness in a life of trust and joy, we shall receive the power to prove, even in the body, how fully and wholly we are in Him who is made unto us sanctification. We shall prove how real and true the holiness of God is in His people.

Prayer

Blessed Lord, who art my sanctification, I come to you now with a very special request. In your own body, you bore our sins on the tree, and it is written of you, "We have been sanctified through the offering of the body of Jesus Christ once for all," so please reveal to me how my body may experience to the full the power of your wonderful redemption. I desire in soul and body to be holy to the Lord.

Lord, I did not understand that my body is the temple of the Holy Spirit and that nothing in it can be a matter of indifference, that its every state and function is to be holiness to the Lord. And where I saw that this should be so, still I sought to guard these walls of the city from the enemy's attacks by myself. I forgot that this part of my being too could be kept and sanctified only by faith, by your taking charge and keeping what faith entrusted to you.

Lord Jesus, I come now to surrender this body with all its needs into your hands. In weariness and nervousness, in excitement and enjoyment, in hunger and want, in health and plenty, O holy Savior, let my body be in your keeping every moment. You call us, "being made free from sin, to present our members as servants of righteousnes unto sanctification."

*Savior, by faith in the freedom from sin which I have in you,
I present every member of my body to you: I believe the Spirit
of life in you makes me free from the law of sin in my members.
Whether living or dying, magnify yourself in my body. Amen.*

Personal Application

1. In the tabernacle and temple, the material part was to be in harmony with, and the embodiment of, the holiness that dwelt within. It was therefore all made according to the pattern shown in the mount. In the two last chapters of Exodus, we have eighteen times "as the Lord commanded." Everything, even in the exterior, was the embodiment of the will of God. Even so our body, as God's temple, must in everything be regulated by God's Word, quickened and sanctified by the Holy Spirit.

2. As part of this holiness in the body, Scripture mentions dress. Speaking of the "outward adorning of plaiting the hair, of wearing jewels, or the putting on of apparel," as inconsistent with "the apparel of a meek and quiet spirit," Peter says, "After this manner aforetime the holy women, who hoped in God, adorned themselves." Holiness was seen in their dress; their body was the temple of the Holy Spirit.

3. "If ye through the Spirit do make dead the deeds of the body, ye shall live." His quickening energy must reign through the whole. We are so accustomed to connect the spiritual with the ideal and invisible that it will need time and thought and faith to realize how the physical and the sensible influence our spiritual life, and must be under the mastery and inspiration of God's Spirit. Even Paul says, "I buffet my body, and bring it into bondage, lest I myself should be rejected."

4. If God actually breathed His Spirit into the body of Adam formed out of the ground, let it not be thought strange that the Holy Spirit should now animate our bodies too with His sanctifying energy.

5. "Corporeality is the end of the ways of God." This deep saying of an old divine reminds us of a much neglected truth. The great work of God's Spirit is to ally himself with matter and form it into a spiritual body for a dwelling for God. In

our body the Holy Spirit will do it if He gets complete possession.

6. It is on this truth of the Holy Spirit's power in the body that what is called faith healing rests. Through all ages, in times of special spiritual quickening, God has allowed some to see how Christ would make, even here, the body partaker of the life and power of the Spirit. To those who do see it, the link between holiness and healing is a very close and blessed one as the Lord Jesus takes possession of the body for himself.

CHAPTER TWENTY-FOUR

Holiness and Cleansing

"Having therefore these promises, dearly beloved, let us cleanse ourselves from all filthiness of the flesh and spirit, perfecting holiness in the fear of God" (2 Cor. 7:1).

That holiness is more than cleansing, and must be preceded by it, is taught in more than one passage of the New Testament. "Christ loved the church, and gave himself up for it, that he might sanctify it, having cleansed it by the washing of water with the word." "If a man cleanse himself from these, he shall be a vessel sanctified." The cleansing is the negative side, the being separate and not touching the unclean thing, the removal of impurity; the sanctifying is the positive union and fellowship with God, and the participation of the graces of the divine life and holiness (2 Cor. 6:17, 18). So we read too of the altar, that God said to Moses: "Thou shalt cleanse the altar, when thou hast made atonement for it, and thou shalt anoint it, to sanctify it" (Ex. 29:36). Cleansing must ever prepare the way, and ought always to lead on to holiness.

Paul speaks of a twofold defilement, of flesh and spirit, from which we must cleanse ourselves. The connection between the two is so close that in every sin both are partakers. The lowest and most carnal form of sin will enter the spirit, and, dragging it down into partnership in crime, will defile and degrade it. And so will all defilement of spirit in course of time show its power in the flesh. Still we may speak of the two classes of sins depending on whether they trace their origin more directly to the flesh or the spirit.

"Let us cleanse ourselves from all defilement of the flesh." The functions of our body may be categorized under three heads: the nourishment, the propagation, and the protection of our life. Through the first the world daily appeals to our appetite with its food and drink. As the fruit good for food was the temptation that overcame Eve, so the pleasures of eating and drinking are among the earliest forms of defilement of the flesh. Closely connected with this are the functions of the second category, those which in Scripture are especially connected with the word flesh. We know how in Paradise the sinful eating was at once followed by the awakening of sinful lust and of shame. In Corinthians, Paul closely connects the two (1 Cor. 6:13, 15), as he also links drunkenness and impurity (1 Cor. 6:9, 10). Then comes the third category in which the vitality of the body displays itself: the instinct of self-preservation, setting itself against everything that interferes with our pleasures and comfort. What is called temper, with its fruits of anger and strife, has its roots in the physical constitution and is one among the sins of the flesh. From all this, the Christian who would be holy must resolutely cleanse himself. He must yield himself to the searching of God's Spirit to be taught what there is in the flesh that is not in harmony with the temperance and self-control demanded both by the law of nature and the law of the Spirit. He must believe what Paul felt the Corinthians so emphatically needed to be taught, that the Holy Spirit dwells in the body, making its members the members of Christ; and in this faith he must put off the works of the flesh; he must cleanse himself from all defilement of flesh.

"And spirit." Just as the source of all defilement of the flesh is self-gratification, so self-seeking is at the root of all defilement of the spirit. In relation to God, it manifests itself in idolatry, whether in the worship of other gods after our own heart, the love of the world more than God, or the doing our will rather than His. In relation to our fellowmen, it shows itself in envy, hatred and want of love, cold neglect or harsh judging of others. In relation to ourselves, it is seen as pride, ambition or envy, the disposition that makes self the center around which all must move and by which all must be judged.

For the discovery of such defilement of spirit, no less than of the sins of the flesh, the believer needs the light of the Holy Spirit so that the uncleanness may indeed be cleansed and cast away forever. Even unconscious sin, if we are not earnestly willing to have it shown to us, will most effectually prevent our progress in the path of holiness.

"Beloved! let us cleanse ourselves." The cleansing is sometimes spoken of as the work of God (Acts 15:9; 1 John 1:9); sometimes as that of Christ (John 15:3; Eph. 5:26; Titus 2:14). Here we are commanded to cleanse ourselves. God does His work in us by the Holy Spirit. The Holy Spirit does His work by stirring us up and enabling us to do it. The Spirit is the strength of the new life; in that strength we must set ourselves determinedly to cast out whatever is unclean. "Come out, and be ye separate, and touch not the unclean thing." It is not only doing what is sinful and willing it that the Christian must avoid, but even touching it. The involuntary contact with it must be so unbearable as to force the cry, "O wretched man that I am!" and to lead on to the deliverance which the Spirit of the life of Christ does bring.

How is this cleansing to be done? When Hezekiah called the priests to sanctify the temple that had been defiled, we read, "The priests went in unto the inner part of the house of the Lord to cleanse it, and brought out all the uncleanness that they found" (2 Chron. 29). Only then could the sin offering of atonement and the burnt offering of consecration, with the thank offerings, be brought, and God's service be restored. In this way all that is unclean must be searched out, and brought out to the light and utterly cast out. However deeply rooted the sin may appear, rooted in constitution and habit, we must cleanse ourselves of it if we would be holy. "If we walk in the light, as he is in the light, the blood of Jesus Christ cleanseth from all sin." As we bring out every sin from the inner part of the house into the light of God and walk in the light, the precious blood that justifies will work mightily to cleanse also. The blood brings it into living contact with the life and the love of God. Let us come into the light with the sin. The blood will prove its mighty power. Let us cleanse ourselves by yielding ourselves to the light to reveal and condemn, to the blood to cleanse and sanctify.

"Let us cleanse ourselves, . . . perfecting holiness in the fear of God." We read in Heb. 10:14, "[Christ] hath perfected for ever them that are sanctified." We have often seen that what God has made holy, man must make holy too as he accepts and appropriates the holiness God has bestowed. So it is here with the perfection which the saints have in Christ. We must perfect holiness: holiness must be carried out into the whole of life, and carried on even to its end. As God's holy ones, we must go on to perfection, perfecting holiness. Do not let us be afraid of the expression. Our Blessed Lord used it when He gave us the command, "Be ye perfect, even as your Father in heaven is perfect." A child striving after perfection in knowledge of his profession, which he hopes to attain when he has finished school, is told by his teacher that the way to the perfection he hopes for at the end of his course is to seek to be perfect in the lessons of each day. To be perfect in the small portion of the work that each hour brings is the path to the perfection that will crown the whole. The Master calls us to a perfection like that of the Father. He has already perfected us in himself. He holds out the prospect of ever-growing perfection. His Word tells us here day by day to be perfecting holiness. Let us seek in each duty to be whole-hearted and complete. As teachable scholars, let us in every act of worship or obedience, in every temptation and trial, do the very best which God's Spirit can enable us to do. "Let patience have its perfect work, that ye may be perfect and entire, lacking in nothing." "The God of peace make you perfect in every good work to do his will."

"Having therefore these promises, dearly beloved, let us cleanse ourselves from all filthiness of the flesh and spirit, perfecting holiness in the fear of God." Faith gives the courage and the power to cleanse from all defilement, perfecting holiness in the fear of God. As the promises of the divine love and indwelling (2 Cor. 6:16–18) are made ours by the Holy Spirit, we shall share the victory which overcomes the world, even our faith. In the path along which we have already come, from the rest in Paradise down through Holy Scripture, we have seen the wondrous revelation of these promises in ever-growing splendor. God the Holy One will make us holy. God the Holy One will dwell with the lowly. God in His

Holy One has come to be our holiness. God has planted us in Christ that He may be our sanctification. God, who chose us in sanctification of the Spirit, has given us the Holy Spirit in our hearts, and now watches over us in His love to work out through the Spirit His purposes and perfect our holiness. Such are the promises that have been set before us. "Having therefore these promises, dearly beloved, let us cleanse ourselves from all filthiness of the flesh and spirit, perfecting holiness in the fear of God."

Beloved brother, here see God's way of holiness. Arise and step onto it in the faith of the promise, fully persuaded that what He has promised He is mighty to perform. Bring out of the inner part of the house all uncleanness. Bring it into the light of God. Confess it and cast it at His feet, who takes it away and cleanses you in His blood. In Christ your strength, yield yourself in faith to perfect the holiness to which you are called. As your Father in heaven is perfect, give yourself to Him as a little child to be perfect too in your daily lessons and your daily walk. Believe that your surrender is accepted, that the charge committed to Him is undertaken. And give glory to Him who is able to do above what you can ask or think.

Prayer

Holy Lord Jesus, you gave yourself for us, so that after cleansing us for yourself as your own, you might sanctify us and present us to yourself a glorious Church, not having spot or wrinkle or any such thing. Blessed by your name for that wonderful love. Blessed be your name for the wonderful cleansing. Through the washing by the Word and the washing in the blood, you have made us every bit clean. And as we walk in the light, you cleanse every moment.

Armed with these promises and in the power of your Word and blood, you call us to cleanse ourselves from all defilement of flesh and spirit. Blessed Lord, graciously reveal in your holy light all that is defilement, even its most secret working. Let me live as one who is to be presented to you without spot or wrinkle or any such thing—cleansed with a divine cleansing, because you gave yourself to do it. Under the living power of your Word and blood, applied by the Holy Spirit, let my way be clean, and my hands clean, my lips clean, and my heart clean. Cleanse me thoroughly that I may walk with you in white here on earth, keeping my garments unspotted and undefiled. For your great love's sake, my Blessed Lord. Amen.

Personal Application

1. Cleansing has almost always one aim: a cleansed vessel is fit for use. Spiritual work done for God, with the honest desire that He may through His Spirit use us, will give urgency to our desire for cleansing. A vessel not cleansed cannot be used. Is not this the reason that there are some workers God cannot bless?

2. All defilement: one stain defiles. "Let us cleanse ourselves from all defilement."

3. No cleansing without light. Open the heart for the light to shine in.

4. No cleansing like fire. Give the defilement over to the fire of His holiness, the fire that consumes and purifies. Give it into the death of Jesus, to Jesus himself.

5. "Perfecting holiness in the fear of God": it is a solemn work. Rejoice with trembling—work out your salvation with fear and trembling.

6. "Having these promises," it is a blessed work to cleanse ourselves—entering into the promises, the purity, the love of our Lord. The fear of God need never hinder the faith in Him. And true faith will never hinder the practical work of cleansing.

7. If we walk in the light, the blood cleanseth. The light reveals; we confess and forsake and accept the blood; so we cleanse ourselves. Let there be a very determined purpose to be clean from all defilement, everything that our Father considers a stain.

CHAPTER TWENTY-FIVE

Holy and Blameless

"Ye are witnesses, and God also, how holily and justly and un-blameably we behaved ourselves among you that believe. The Lord make you to increase and abound in love one toward another, and toward all men . . . to the end he may stablish your hearts unblameable in holiness before God, even our Father, at the coming of our Lord Jesus Christ with all his saints" (1 Thess. 2:10; 3:12, 13).

"He hath chosen us in him before the foundation of the world, that we should be holy and without blame before him in love" (Eph. 1:4).

Two Greek words, signifying nearly the same, are used frequently along with the word holy, and following it, to express what the result and effect of holiness will be as manifested in the visible life. The one is translated without blemish, spotless, and is that also used of our Lord and His sacrifice: the Lamb without blemish (Heb. 9:14; 1 Pet. 1:19). It is then used of God's children with holy—holy and without blemish (Eph. 1:4; 5:27; Col. 1:22; Phil. 2:15; Jude 24; 2 Pet. 3:14). The other word is translated without blame, faultless (as in Luke 1:6; Phil. 2:15; 3:6), and is also found in conjunction with holy (1 Thess. 2:10; 3:13, 23). In answer to the question as to whether this blamelessness has reference to God's estimate of the saints or men's, Scripture clearly connects it with both. In some passages (Eph. 1:4; 5:27; Col. 1:22; 1 Thess. 3:13; 2 Pet. 3:14) the words "before him," "to himself," "before our God and Father" indicate that the first

164

thought is of the spotlessness and faultlessness in the presence of a Holy God, which is held out to us as His purpose and our privilege. In others (such as Phil. 2:15; 1 Thess. 2:10), the blamelessness in the sight of men stands in the foreground. In each case the word may be considered to include both aspects: without blemish and without blame must stand the double test of the judgment of God and man too.

What special lesson does the linking together of these two words in Scripture, and the exposition of holy by the addition of blameless, mean to teach us? A lesson of deep importance. In the pursuit of holiness, the believer faces a danger. The more clearly he realizes what a deep spiritual blessing it is to be found only in separation from the world and direct fellowship with God, to be possessed fully only through a real divine indwelling, the more danger he faces of looking too exclusively to the divine side of the blessing in its heavenly and supernatural aspect. He may forget how repentance and obedience, as the path leading up to holiness, must cover every detail—even the minutest—of daily life. He may not see that faithfulness to the leadings of the Spirit, in such measure as we have Him already, faithfulness to His faintest whisper in reference to ordinary conduct, is essential—if we are to go on to all fuller experience of His power and work as the Spirit of holiness.

But the believer may not have learned that more than obedience to what he knows to be God's will is necessary. He also needs a very tender and willing teachableness to receive all that the Spirit has to show him of his imperfections and the Father's perfect will concerning him. That teachableness is the only condition on which the holiness of God can be more fully revealed to us and in us.

So we see that while the believer is more intent on trying to discover the secret of true and full holiness from the divine side, he may be tolerating glaring faults obvious to all around him. Because of the lack of perfect teachableness—which is sin—he may remain ignorant of graces and beauties of holiness with which the Father would have him make the doctrine of holiness compellingly attractive before men. He may seek to live a very holy life but still not seek a perfectly blameless life.

There have been such saints—holy but hard, holy but

distant, holy but sharp in their judgments of others; holy in men's eyes, but unloving and selfish. The half-heathen Samaritan was more kind and self-sacrificing than the holy Levite and priest. Even though this may be true, it is not the teaching of Holy Scripture that is at fault. In linking holy and without blemish (or without blame) so closely, the Holy Spirit leads us to seek for the embodiment of holiness as a spiritual power in the blamelessness of practice and of daily life. Let every believer who rejoices in God's declaration that he is holy in Christ seek also to perfect holiness and reach out after nothing less than to be "unblameable in holiness."

That this blamelessness has particular reference to our relationship with our fellowmen we see from the way in which it is linked with love. So in Eph. 1:4, "That we should be holy and without blame before him in love." But especially in that remarkable passage, "The Lord make you to increase and abound in love one toward another, and toward all men . . . to the end he may establish your hearts unblameable in holiness." The holiness (the positive hidden divine life principle), and the blameless (the external and human life practice)—both are to find their strength, by which we are to be established in them, in our abounding and ever-flowing love.

Holiness and lovingness—it is of deep importance that these words be inseparably linked in our minds, as their reality should be in our lives. We have seen, in the study of the holiness of God, how love is the element in which it dwells and works, drawing to itself and making like itself all it can get possession of. Of the fire of divine holiness love is the beautiful flame, reaching out to communicate itself and assimilate to itself all it can grasp. In God's children true holiness is the same: the divine fire burns to bring into its own blessedness all that comes within its reach. When Jesus sanctified himself that we might be sanctified in truth, that was love giving itself to the death that the sinful might share His holiness. Selfishness and holiness are irreconcilable. Ignorance may think of sanctity as a beautiful garment with which to adorn itself before God, while underneath there is a selfish pride saying, "I am holier than thou," and quite content that the other should lack that which it possesses. On the contrary, true holiness is the expulsion and the death of selfishness. Holiness takes possession of heart and life to be the ministers of that fire of love that consumes itself, to reach and purify and save others. Holiness is love. Abounding love is what Paul prays for as the condition of unblamable holiness. It is as the Lord makes us increase and abound in love that He can establish our hearts unblamable in holiness.

The Apostle speaks of a twofold love, "love toward each other, and toward all men." Love to the brethren was what our Lord himself required as the salient mark of discipleship. And He prayed the Father for it as the principal proof to the world of the truth of His divine mission. It is in the holiness of love, in a loving holiness, that the unity of the body will be proved and promoted and prepared for the fuller workings of the Holy Spirit. In Corinthians and Galatians, division and distance between believers are named as sure proof of the life of self and the flesh. If we would be holy, begin by being very gentle and patient, forgiving and kind, and generous in our relationships with all the Father's children. Study the divine image of the love that seeks not its own. Pray unceasingly that the Lord may make us abound in love to each other. The holiest will be humblest and most self-forgetting, the gentlest and most self-denying, the kindest and most thoughtful of others for Jesus' sake. "Put on therefore, as God's elect, holy and beloved, a heart of compassion, kindness, lowliness, meekness, long-suffering" (Col. 3:12, 13, ASV).

The love toward all men is a love proved in the course and conduct of daily life. A love that not only avoids anger and evil temper and harsh judgments, but exhibits the more positive virtue of active devotion to the welfare and interests of all. A charitable love that cares for the bodies as well as the souls. A love that not only is ready to help when it is called, but that really gives itself up to self-denial and self-sacrifice to discover and relieve the needs of the most wretched and unworthy. A love that truly takes Christ's love—that brought Him from heaven and led Him to choose the cross—as the only law and measure for its conduct, and makes everything subordinate to the Godlike blessedness of giving, of doing good, of embracing and saving the needy and lost. Thus abounding in love, we shall be unblamable in holiness.

In Christ we are holy; of God we are in Christ, who is made of God unto us sanctification. In this faith Paul prays that the Lord, our Lord Jesus, may make us increase and abound in love. The Father is the fountain; Jesus Christ is the channel; the Holy Spirit is the living stream. And the Lord Jesus is our life, through the Spirit. By faith in Him, by abiding in Him and in His love, by allowing—in close union with Christ—the Spirit to shed abroad the love of God, we shall receive the answer to our prayer, and shall by Him be established unblamable in holiness. Pray in a faith that changes into praise: Blessed be the Lord, who will make us increase and abound in love, and will establish us unblamable in holiness before our God and Father, at the coming of our Lord Jesus with His holy ones.

Prayer

Most Gracious God and Father, again I thank you for that wondrous salvation, through sanctification of the Spirit, which has made us holy in Christ. I thank you that the Spirit can so make us partakers of the life of Christ that we too may be unblamable in holiness. I thank you that the Lord himself makes us increase and abound in love, and makes our hearts steadfast in this abounding love and unblamable holiness.

Blessed Lord and Savior, I come now to claim and take as my own all that you are able to do for me. I am holy only in you; in you I am holy. In you there is the power for me to abound in love. O Lord, my Lord, in whom the fullness of God's love abides and in whom I abide, make me to abound in love. In union with you, in the life of faith in which you live in me, it can be and it shall be. By the teaching of your Holy Spirit lead me in all footsteps of your self-denying love that I too may be consumed in blessing others.

And thus, Lord, mightily establish my heart to be unblamable in holiness. Let self perish before your presence. Let your holiness, giving itself to make the sinner holy, take entire possession until my heart and life are sanctified wholly, and my whole spirit and soul and body be preserved blameless unto your coming. Amen.

Personal Application

1. Let us pray very earnestly that our interest in the study of holiness may not be a thing of the intellect or the emotions, but of the will and the life, seen of all men in the daily walk and conversation. "Abounding in love," "unblamable in holiness," will give favor with God and man.

2. "God is love"; creation is the outflow of love. Redemption is the sacrifice and the triumph of love. Holiness is the fire of love. The beauty of the life of Jesus is love. All we enjoy of the divine we owe to love. Our holiness is not God's, is not Christ's, if we do not love.

3. "Love seeketh not its own." "Love never faileth." "Love is the fulfilling of the law." "The greatest of these is love." "The end of the commandment is love." To love God and man is to be holy. In the course of daily life, holiness can have its simple and sweet beginnings and its exercise; so, in its highest attainment, holiness is love made perfect.

4. Faith has all its worth from love, from the love of God from which it draws and drinks, and the love to God and man which streams out of it. Let us be strong in faith; then shall we abound in love.

5. "The love of God hath been shed abroad in our hearts by the Holy Ghost which was given unto us." Let this be our confidence.

CHAPTER TWENTY-SIX

Holiness and the Will of God

"For this is the will of God, even your sanctification" (1 Thess. 4:3).

"Lo, I come to do thy will. . . . By the which will we are sanctified, through the offering of the body of Jesus Christ once for all" (Heb. 10:9, 10).

In the will of God we have the union of His wisdom and power. Wisdom decides and declares what is to be. Power secures the performance. The declarative will is only one side; its complement, the executive will, is the living energy in which everything good has its origin and existence. So long as we only look at the will of God in the former light, as law, we feel it a burden, because we have not the power to perform—it is too high for us. But when faith looks to the power that works in God's will and carries it out, then faith has the courage to accept and fulfill God's will because it knows God himself is working it out. The surrender in faith to the divine will as wisdom thus becomes the pathway to the experience of it as a power. "He doeth according to his will," then, is the expression not of forced submission only, but of joyful expectation.

"This is the will of God . . . your sanctification." Ordinarily, these words are simply taken to mean that, among many other things that God has willed, sanctification is one; it is something in accordance with His will. This thought contains teaching of great value. God distinctly and definitely has willed your sanctification. Your sanctification has its source and certainty in its being God's will. We are "elect in sanctification of the Spirit" and "chosen to be holy"; the purpose of God's will from eternity, and His will now, is our sanctification. Only think about God's will being a divine power that works out what His wisdom has chosen and see how this truth will strengthen our faith that we shall be holy. God wills it, and will work it out for all and in all who do not resist but yield themselves to its power. Seek your sanctification, not only in the will of God, as a declaration of what He wants you to be, but as a revelation of what He himself will work out in you.

There is, however, another wonderful thought suggested. If our sanctification be God's will, its central thought and its contents, every part of that will must bear upon it, and the sure entrance to sanctification will be the hearty acceptance of the will of God in all things. To be one with God's will is to be holy. Let him who would be holy take his place here and "stand in all the will of God." He will there meet God himself, and be made partaker of His holiness, because His will works out its purpose in power to each one who yields himself to it. Everything in a life of holiness depends upon our being in the right relation to the will of God.

Many Christians think it impossible to accept all the will of God or to be one with it. They look upon the will of God in its thousand commands and its numberless providential orderings. Sometimes they have found it extremely hard to obey even one single command, or to bear willingly some light disappointment. They imagine that they would need to be a thousandfold holier and stronger in grace before venturing to say that they do accept all God's will, whether to do or to bear. They cannot understand that all the difficulty comes from their not occupying the right point of view. They are looking at God's will as at variance with their natural will, and they feel that that natural will will never delight in all of God's will. They forget that the new man has a renewed will. This new will delights in the will of God because it is born of it. This new will sees the beauty and the glory of God's will and is in harmony with it. If they are indeed God's children, the very first impulse of the spirit of a child is surely to do the will of the Father in heaven. And they have only to yield themselves heartily and wholly to this spirit of sonship, and they need not fear to accept God's will as theirs.

The mistake they make is a very serious one. Instead of living by faith they judge by feeling, in which the old nature speaks and rules. It tells them that God's will is often a burden too hard to be borne, and that they never can have the strength to do it. Faith speaks differently. It reminds us that God is love and that His will is nothing but love revealed. It asks if we do not know that there is nothing more perfect or beautiful in heaven or earth than the will of God. It shows us how in our conversion we have already professed to accept God as Father and Lord. It assures us, above all, that if we will but definitely and trustingly give ourselves to that will which is love, it will as love fill our hearts and make us delight in it, and so become the power that enables us to do and to bear joyfully. Faith reveals to us that the will of God is the power of His love, working out its plan in divine beauty in each one who wholly yields to it.

Which shall we choose? Where shall we take our place? Shall we attempt to accept Christ as a Savior without accepting His will? Shall we profess to be the Father's children, and still spend our life in debating how much of His will we shall perform? Shall we be content to go on from day to day with the painful consciousness that our will is not in harmony with God's will? Or shall we at once and forever give up our will as sinful to His—to that will which He has already written on our heart? This surrender is possible. It can be made. In a simple, definite transaction with God, we can say that we do accept His holy will to be ours. Faith knows that God will not pass such a surrender unnoticed, but will accept it. In the trust that He now takes us up into His will, and undertakes to breathe it into us, with the love and the power to perform it—in this faith let us enter into God's will and begin a new life, standing in, abiding in the very center of this most holy will.

Such an acceptance of God's will prepares the believer, through the Holy Spirit, to recognize and know that will in whatever form it comes. The great difference between the carnal and the spiritual Christian is that the latter acknowledges God, under whatever low and poor and human appearances He manifests himself. When God comes in trials which can be traced to no hand but His, he says, "Thy will be done." When trials come through the weakness of men or his own folly, when circumstances appear unfavorable to his religious progress, and temptations threaten to be too much for him and to overcome him, he learns first of all to see God in everything, and still to say, "Thy will be done." He knows that a child of God cannot possibly be in any situation without the will of His heavenly Father, even when that will has been to leave him to his own willfullness for a time, or to suffer the consequences of his own or others' sin. He sees this, and in accepting his circumstances as the will of God to try and prove him, he is in the right position for now knowing and doing what is right. Seeing and honoring God's will thus in everything, he learns always to abide in that will.

He does so also by doing that will. As his spiritual discernment grows to be able to say of whatever happens, "All things are of God," so he grows too in wisdom and spiritual understanding to know the will of God as it is to be done. In the indications of conscience and of Providence, in the teaching of the Word and the Spirit, he learns to see how God's will has reference to every part and every duty of life, and it becomes his joy in all things to live, "doing the will of God from the heart, as unto the Lord and not unto men." "Labouring fervently in prayer to stand complete and fully assured in all the will of God," he finds how blessedly the Father has accepted his surrender, and supplies all the light and strength that is needed that His will may be done by him on earth as it is in heaven.

Have you indeed given yourself to this Holy God for Him to make you holy? Have you accepted and entered into the good and perfect will of God? Are you living in it? The question is not, whether, when affliction comes, you accept the inevitable and submit to a will you cannot resist; but whether you have chosen the will of God as your chief good, and have taken the life principle of Christ to be yours: "I delight to do thy will, O God." This was the holiness of Christ, in which He sanctified himself and us, the doing God's will. "In which will we have been sanctified." It is this will of God which is our sanctification.

Do you truly want to be holy? To be wholly possessed of God? Here is the path. I plead with you not to be afraid or to hold back. You have taken God to be your God; have you really taken His will to be your will? Oh, think of the privilege, the blessedness, of having one will with God! Fear not the surrender of yourself to it most unreservedly. The will of God is, in every part of it, and in all its divine power, your sanctification.

Prayer

Blessed Father, I come to say that I see that your will is my sanctification, and alone I will seek it. Graciously grant that, by your Holy Spirit which dwells in me, the glory of that will, and the blessedness of abiding in it, may be fully revealed to me.

Teach me to know it as the will of Love, purposing always what is the very best and most blessed for your child. Teach me to know it as the will of Omnipotence, able to work out its every counsel in me. Teach me to know it in Christ, fulfilled perfectly on my behalf. Teach me to know it as what the Spirit wills and works in each one who yields to Him.

O my Father, I acknowledge your claim to have your will alone done, and am here for it to do with me as you please. With my whole heart I enter into it, to be one with it forever. Your Holy Spirit can maintain this oneness without interruption. I trust you, my Father, step by step, to let the light of your will shine in my heart and on my path, through that Spirit.

May this be the holiness in which I live, that I forget and lose self in pleasing and honoring you. Amen.

Personal Application

1. Make it a study, in meditation and prayer and worship, to get a full impression of the majesty, the perfection, the glory of the will of God, with the privilege and possibility of living in it.

2. Study it, too, as the expression of an infinite love and fatherliness; its every manifestation full of lovingkindness. Every providence is God's will; whatever happens, meet God

in it in humble worship. Every precept is God's will; meet God in it with loving obedience. Every promise is God's will; meet God in it with full trust. A life in the will of God is rest and strength and blessing.

3. Above all, forget not to believe in its omnipotent power. He works all things after the counsel of His will. In nature and those who resist Him, without their consent. In His children, according to their faith and as far as they will it. Do believe that the will of God will work out its counsel in you, as you trust it to do so.

4. This will is infinite benevolence and beneficence revealed in the self-sacrifice of Jesus. Live for others: so can you become an instrument for the divine will to use (Matt. 18:14; John 6:39, 40). Yield yourselves to this redeeming will of God that it may get full possession, and work out through you, too, its saving purpose.

5. Christ is just the embodiment of God's will: He is God's will done. Abide in Him by abiding in, by doing heartily and always, the will of God. A Christian is, like Christ, a man given up to the will of God.

CHAPTER TWENTY-SEVEN

Holiness and Service

"If a man therefore purge himself from these, he shall be a vessel unto honour, sanctified, and meet for the master's use, and prepared unto every good work" (2 Tim. 2:21).

"An holy priesthood, to offer up spiritual sacrifices. . . . An holy nation, that ye should shew forth the praises of him who hath called you out of darkness into his marvellous light" (1 Pet. 2:5, 9).

Through the whole of Scripture we have seen that whatever God sanctifies is to be used in the service of His holiness. His holiness is an infinite energy that only finds its rest in making holy. To the revelation of what He is in himself, "I the Lord am holy," God continually adds the declaration of what He does, "I am the Lord that make holy." Holiness is a burning fire that extends itself, that seeks to consume what is unholy, and to communicate its own blessedness to all that will receive it. Holiness and selfishness, holiness and inactivity, holiness and sloth, holiness and helplessness, are utterly irreconcilable. Whatever we read of as holy was taken into the service of the holiness of God.

What was revealed as holy in Scripture? The seventh day was made holy that in it God might make His people holy. The tabernacle was holy to serve as a dwelling for the Holy One, as the center from which His holiness might manifest itself to the people. The altar was most holy that it might sanctify the gifts laid on it. The priests with their garments, the house with its furniture and vessels, the sacrifices and the blood—whatever bore the name of holy had a use and a purpose. Of Israel, whom God redeemed from Egypt that they might be a holy nation, God said, "Let my people go, that they may serve me." The holy angels, the holy prophets and apostles, the holy Scriptures—all bore the title as having been sanctified for the service of God. Our Lord speaks of himself "as the Son, whom the Father sanctified and sent into the world." And when He says, "I sanctify myself," He adds at once the purpose: it is in the service of the Father and His redeemed ones "that they also may be sanctified through the truth."

Could it be possible, now that God, in Christ the Holy One and in the Holy Spirit, is accomplishing His purpose—gathering a people of saints, "holy ones," "made holy in Christ"—that now holiness and service would be cast aside? Impossible! First we shall see how essential they are to each other. Let us try to grasp the mutual relationship—we are made holy only that we may serve. We can serve only as we are holy.

Holiness is essential to effectual service. In the Old Testament we see degrees of holiness, not only in the holy places, but also in holy people. There is an advance from step to step: in the nation, the Levites, the priests, and then the high priest. As in each succeeding stage the circle narrows and the service is more refined and distinct, so the holiness required is more refined and more distinct. This is also true in this more spiritual dispensation: the more of holiness, the greater the fitness for service. The more there is of true holiness, the more there is of God, and the truer and deeper is the entrance He has had into the soul. The hold He has on the soul to use it in His service is more complete.

In the Church of Christ there is a vast amount of work done which yields very little fruit. Many throw themselves into work although they have but little true holiness, little of the Holy Spirit. They often work most diligently, and, as far as human influence is concerned, most successfully. And yet true spiritual results in the building up of a holy temple in the Lord are but few. The Lord cannot work in them because He does not rule their inner life. His personal indwelling and fellowship, the rest of His holy presence, His holiness reigning and ruling in the heart and life—to all these they are comparative strangers. It has been rightly said that work is the cure for spiritual poverty and disease; to some believers who had been seeking holiness apart from service, the call to work has been an unspeakable blessing. But to many it has been only an additional blind to cover up the terrible lack of heart holiness and heart fellowship with the living God. They have thrown themselves into work more earnestly than ever, and yet have not in their heart the rest-giving and refreshing witness that their work is acceptable and accepted.

"If a man cleanse himself, he shall be a vessel unto honour, sanctified, meet for the Master's use, prepared unto every good work." You cannot have the law of service more clearly or beautifully laid down. A vessel of honor, one whom the King will delight to honor, must be a vessel cleansed from all defilement of flesh and spirit. Only then can it be a sanctified vessel, possessed and indwelt by God's Holy Spirit. So it becomes meet for the Master's use. He can use it, work in it and wield it. And so, clean and holy, yielded into the Master's hands, we are divinely prepared for every good work. Holiness is essential to service. If our service is to be acceptable to God and effectual in its work with souls, and is to be a joy and a strength to us ourselves, we must be holy. The will of God must first live in us if it is to be done by us.

How many faithful workers there are, mourning the want of power, longing and praying for it, and yet not obtaining it! They have spent their strength more in the outer court of work and service than in the inner life of fellowship and faith. They truly have never understood that only as the Master gets possession of them, as the Holy Spirit has them at His disposal, can He use them, can they have true power. They often long and cry for what they call a baptism of power. They forget that the way to have God's power in us is for us to be in His power. Put yourself into the power of God. Let His holy will live in you; live in it and in obedience to it as one who has no power to dispose of himself. Let the Holy Spirit dwell within, as in His holy temple, revealing the Holy One on the throne ruling all. Without fail He will use you as a vessel of honor, sanctified and meet for the Master's use. Holiness is essential to effectual service.

Service is *equally* essential to true holiness. Holiness is an energy, an intense energy of desire and self-sacrifice, to make others partakers of its own purity and perfection. Christ sacrificed himself—of what did that sacrifice consist, and what was its aim? He sanctified himself that we might be sanctified too. A holiness that is selfish is a delusion. True holiness, God's holiness in us, works itself out in love, in seeking and loving the unholy, that they may become holy too. Self-sacrificing love is the very essence of holiness. The Holy One of Israel is its Redeemer. The Holy One of God is the dying Savior. The Holy Spirit of God makes holy. There is no holiness in God except that which is most actively engaged in loving and saving and blessing. It must be so in us too. Let every thought of holiness, every act of faith or prayer, every effort in pursuit of it, be animated by the desire and the surrender of its object. Let your whole life be one distinctly and definitely surrendered to God for His use and service. Your circumstances may appear to be unfavorable. God may appear to keep the door closed against your working for Him in the way you would wish; your sense of unfitness may be painful. Even so let the matter be settled between God and your soul: your longing for holiness is so that you may be better fitted for Him to use, and what He has given you of His holiness in Christ and the Spirit is all at His disposal, waiting to be used. Be ready for Him to use, live out, in a daily life of humble, self-denying, loving service of others, what grace you have received. You will find that in the union and interchange of worship and work, God's holiness will rest upon you.

"The Father sanctified the Son, and sent him into the world." The world is the place for the sanctified one, to be its light, its salt, its life. We are "sanctified in Christ Jesus," and sent into the world too. Let us not be afraid to accept our position, our double position—in the world and in Christ! In the world, with its sin and sorrow, with its thousands of needs touching us at every point, and its millions of souls all waiting for us. And in Christ too. For the sake of that world we "have been sanctified in Christ"; we are "holy in Christ"; we have "the spirit of sanctification" dwelling in us. As a holy salt in a sinful world, let us give ourselves to our holy calling. Let us come nearer and nearer to God who has called us. Let us root deeper and deeper in Christ our sanctification, in whom we are of God. Let us enter more firmly and more fully into that faith in Him in whom we are, so that our whole life will be covered and taken up in His. Let us beseech the Father to teach us that His Holy Spirit does dwell in us every moment, making Christ with His holiness, our home, our abode, our sure defense, and our infinite supply. As He which hath called us is holy, let us be holy in His own Son, through His own Spirit, and the fire of His holy love will work through us its work of judging and condemning, of saving and sanctifying. A sanctified soul God will use to save.

Prayer

Blessed Master, I thank you for being reminded again of the purpose of your redeeming love. You gave yourself that you might cleanse for yourself a people of your own, zealous in good works. You would make of each of us a vessel of honor, cleansed and sanctified, meet for your use, and prepared for every good work.

Blessed Lord, write the lessons of your Word deep in my heart. Teach me and all your people that if we would work for you, if we would have you work in us, and use us, we must be very holy, holy as God is holy. And that if we would be holy, we must be serving you. It is your own Spirit, by which you sanctify us to use us and in using sanctify. To be entirely possessed of you is the path to sanctity and service both.

Most Holy Savior, we are in you as our sanctification: in you we would abide. In the rest of a faith that trusts you for all, in the power of a surrender that would have no will but yours, in a love that would lose itself to be wholly yours, Blessed Jesus, we do abide in you. In you we are holy: in you we shall bear much fruit.

Oh, be pleased to perfect your own work in us! Amen.

Personal Application

1. It is difficult to make it clear in words how growth in holiness will simply reveal itself as an increasing simplicity and self-forgetfulness, accompanied by the restful and most blessed assurance that God has complete possession of us and will use us. We pass from the stage in which work presses

as an obligation; it becomes the joy of fruit-bearing; faith's assurance that He is working out His will through us.

2. It has sometimes been said that people might be better employed in working for God than attending holiness conventions. This is surely a misunderstanding. It was before the throne of the Thrice Holy One, and as he heard the seraphim sing of God's holiness, that the prophet said, "Here am I, send me." As the mission of Moses, and Isaiah, and the Son, whom the Father sanctified and sent, each had its origin in the revelation of God's holiness, our missions will receive new power as they are more directly born out of worship of God as the Holy One, and baptized into the Spirit of holiness.

3. Let every worker take time to hear God's double call. If you would work, be very holy. If you would be holy, give yourself to God to use in His work.

4. Note the connection between "sanctified" and "meet for the Master's use." True holiness is being possessed of God; true service being used of God. How much service there is in which we are the chief agents, and ask God to help and to bless us. True service is being yielded up to the Master for Him to use. Then the Holy Spirit is the agent and we are the instruments of His will. Such service is holiness.

5. "I sanctify myself, that they also": a reference to others is the root principle of all true holiness.

CHAPTER TWENTY-EIGHT

The Way into the Holiest

"Having therefore, brethren, boldness to enter into the holiest by the blood of Jesus, by a new and living way, which he hath conse-crated for us, through the veil, that is to say, his flesh; and having an high priest over the house of God; let us draw near with a true heart, in full assurance of faith" (Heb. 10:19–22).

When the high priest once a year entered into the second tabernacle within the veil, it was, we are told in Hebrews, "the Holy Ghost signifying that the way into the holiest of all was not yet made manifest." When Christ died the veil was rent. All who were serving in the holy place had free access at once into the most holy. The way into the holiest of all was opened up. When the epistle passes over to its practical application (10:19), all its teaching is summed up in the words: "Having therefore, brethren, boldness to enter into the holiest . . . let us draw near." Christ's redemption has opened the way to the holiest of all: our acceptance of it must lead to nothing less than our drawing near and enter-ing in. The text suggests four very precious thoughts in re-gard to the place of access, the right of access, the way of access and the power of access.

The place of access. To what place are we invited to draw near? "Having boldness to enter into the holiest." The priests in Israel might enter the holy place, but were always ex-cluded from the holiest, God's immediate presence. The rent veil proclaimed liberty of access into that presence. It is there

182

that believers as a royal priesthood are now to live and walk. Within the veil, in the very holiest of all, in the same place, the heavenlies, in which God dwells, in God's very presence, is to be our abode—our home. Some say "Let us draw near" meant prayer, and that in our special approach to God in acts of worship we enter the holiest. No; as great as this privilege is, God meant something infinitely greater for us. We are to draw near and dwell—live our life and do our work—always within the sphere, the atmosphere, of the inner sanctuary. It is God's presence that makes holy ground; God's immediate presence in Christ makes any place the holiest of all: and it is this which we are to draw near and in which we are to abide. There is not a single moment of the day, there is not a circumstance or surrounding which can block the believer's continual dwelling in the secret place of the Most High. As by faith he enters into the completeness of his reconciliation with God, and the reality of his oneness with Christ, and as he thus, abiding in Christ, yields to the Holy Spirit to reveal within the presence of the Holy One, the holiest of all is around him—he is indeed in it. With an uninterrupted access he draws near.*

The right of access. Is this simply an ideal? Can it be a reality, an experience in daily life to those who know how sinful their nature is? Blessed be God, it is meant to be. It is possible, because our right of access rests not in what we are but in the blood of Jesus. "Having boldness to enter into the holiest by the blood of Jesus, let us draw near." In the Passover we saw how redemption and the holiness it aimed at were dependent on the blood. In the sanctuary, God's dwelling, we know how in each part, the court, the holy place, the most holy, the sprinkling of blood was what alone secured access to God. And now that the blood of Jesus has been shed, what divine power, what intense reality, what everlasting efficacy, we have in gaining access into the holiest of all, the most holy of God's heart and His love! We are indeed brought nigh by the blood. We have boldness to enter by the blood.

---

*So near, so very near to God,
  I cannot nearer be;
For in the person of His Son,
  I am as near as He.

"The worshipers, being once cleansed, have no more conscience of sins." Walking in the light, the blood of Jesus cleanses in the power of an endless life, with a cleansing that never ceases. No consciousness of unworthiness or remaining sinfulness need hinder the boldness of access. The liberty to draw near rests in the never-failing, ever-acting, everliving efficacy of the precious blood. It is possible for a believer to dwell in the holiest of all.

The way of access. It is often thought that the new and living way, dedicated for us by Jesus, means nothing different from the boldness through His blood. This is not the case. The words mean a great deal more. "Having boldness by the blood of Jesus, let us draw near by the way which he dedicated for us." He opened for us a way to walk in, as He walked in it, "a new and living way, through the veil, that is to say, his flesh." The way in which Christ walked when He gave His blood is the very same in which we must walk. That way is the way of the cross. There must not only be faith in Christ's sacrifice, but fellowship with Him in it. That way led to the rending of the veil of the flesh, and so through the rent veil, in to God. And was the veil of Christ's holy flesh rent that the veil of our sinful flesh might be spared? No. He meant us to walk in the very same way in which He did, following closely after Him. He dedicated for us a new and living way through the veil, that is, His flesh. As we go in through the rent veil of His flesh, we find in it at once the need and the power for our flesh to be rent too: following Jesus always means conformity to Jesus. It is Jesus with the rent flesh, in whom we are, in whom we walk.* There is no way to God but through the rending of the flesh. In acceptance of Christ's life and death by faith as the power that works in us, in the power of the Spirit which makes us truly one with Christ, we all follow Christ as He passes on through the rent veil, that is, His flesh, and we become partakers with Him of His crucifixion and death. The way of the cross, "by which I have been crucified," is the way through the rent veil. Man's des-

---

*"Christ suffered, that he might bring us to God, being put to death in the flesh, but quickened in the Spirit." "Forasmuch then as Christ hath suffered for us in the flesh, arm ye yourselves likewise with the same mind." The flesh and the Spirit are antagonistic: as the flesh dies, the Spirit lives.

tiny, fellowship with God in the power of the Holy Spirit, is only reached through the sacrifice of the flesh.

Here we find the solution of a great mystery—why so many Christians stand afar off and never enter this holiest of all; why the holiness of God's presence is so little seen on them. They thought that it was only in Christ that the flesh needed to be rent, not in themselves. They thought that the liberty they had in the blood was the new and living way. They knew not that the way into true and full holiness, into the holiest of all—full entrance into the fellowship of the holiness of the Great High Priest—was only to be reached through the rent veil of the flesh, through conformity to the death of Jesus. This is in very deed the way that He dedicated for us. He is himself the way. Into His self-denial, His self-sacrifice, His crucifixion, He takes up all who long to be holy with His holiness, holy as He is holy.

The power of access. Does anyone shrink back from entering the very holiest for fear of this rending of the flesh because he doubts whether he could bear it, whether he could indeed walk in such a path? Let him listen once more. Hear what follows: "And having an high priest over the house of God, let us draw near." We have not only the holiest of all inviting us, and the blood giving us boldness, and the way through the rent veil consecrated for us, but we have the High Priest over the house of God, the blessed living Savior, to draw, to help, and to welcome us. He is our Aaron. On His heart we see our name, because He only lives to think of us and pray for us. On His forehead we see God's name, "Holy to the Lord," because in His holiness the sins of our best intentions are covered. In Him we are accepted and sanctified; God receives us as holy ones. In the power of His love and His Spirit, in the power of Him the Holy One, in the joy of drawing nearer to Him and being drawn by Him, we gladly accept the way He has dedicated, and walk in His holy footsteps of self-denial and self-sacrifice. We see how the flesh is the thick veil that separates from the Holy One who is a Spirit, and it becomes an unceasing and most fervent prayer that the crucifixion of the flesh may, in the power of the Holy Spirit, be in us a blessed reality. With the glory of the holiest of all shining out on us through the opened veil, and the precious blood speaking so loudly of boldness of access, and the High Priest beckoning us with His loving presence to draw near and be blessed—with all this, we dare no longer fear, but choose the way of the rent veil as the path we love to tread, and give ourselves to enter in and dwell within the veil, in the very holiest of all.

So our life here will be the foretaste of the glory that is promised in four great thoughts of our text—"These are they which came out of great tribulation," that is, by the way of the rent flesh; "and they washed their robes, and made them white in the blood of the Lamb," their boldness through the blood; "therefore are they before the throne of God," their dwelling in the holiest of all; "the Lamb, which is in the midst of the throne, shall be their Shepherd"—the Great Priest still the Shepherd, Jesus himself their all in all.

Do you see what holiness is and how it is to be found? It is not something formed in you. It is not something put on you from without. Holiness is the presence of God resting on you. Holiness comes as you consciously abide in that presence, doing all your work and living all your life as a sacrifice to Him, acceptable through Jesus Christ, sanctified by the Holy Ghost. Do not be fearful that this life is not for you! Look to Jesus. Having a Great High Priest over the house of God, let us draw near. Be occupied with Jesus. Our Brother has charge of the temple; He has liberty to show us all, to lead us into the secret of the Father's presence. The entire management of the temple has been given into His hands with this very purpose, that all the feeble and doubting ones might come with confidence. Only trust yourself to Jesus, to His leading and keeping. Only trust Jesus, God's Holy One, your Holy One; it is His delight to reveal to you what He has purchased with His blood. Trust Him to teach you the ordinance of the sanctuary. "That thou mayest know how thou oughtest to behave thyself in the house of God," He has been given. Having a Great High Priest, let us enter in, let us dwell in the holiest of all. In the power of the blood, in the power of the new and living way, in the power of the living Jesus, let the holiest of all, the presence of God, be the home of our soul. You are "holy in Christ"; in Christ you are in God's holy presence and love; just stay there.

Prayer

Most Holy God, how shall I praise you for the liberty to enter into the holiest of all and dwell there? And for the precious blood that brings us near? And for the new and living way, through the rent veil of that flesh which had separated us from you, in which my flesh now too has been crucified? And for the Great High Priest over the house of God, our living Lord Jesus, with whom and in whom we appear before you? Glory be to your holy name for this wonderful and most complete redemption.

I beseech you, O my God! give me, and all your children, a true concept of the reality that we may live each day, may spend our whole life, within the veil, in your own immediate presence. Give us the spirit of revelation, I pray you, that we may see how the glory of your Presence streams forth through the rent veil from the most holy into the holy place. Show us how, in the pouring out of the Holy Spirit, the kingdom of heaven came to earth, and all who yield themselves to that Spirit may know that in Christ they are indeed so near, so very near to you. O Blessed Father, let your Spirit teach us that this indeed is the holy life: a life in Christ the Holy One, always in the light and the presence of your Holy Majesty.

Most Holy God! I draw nigh. In the power of the Holy Spirit I enter in. I am now in the holiest of all. And here I would abide in Jesus, my Great High Priest—here, in the holiest of all. Amen.

Personal Application

1. To abide in Christ is to dwell in the holiest of all. Christ is not only the sacrifice, and the way, and the Great High Priest, but also himself the temple. "The Lamb is the temple." As the Holy Spirit reveals my union to Christ more clearly, and heart and will lose themselves in Him, I dwell in the holy presence, which is the holiest of all. You are "holy in Christ"—draw near, enter in with boldness, and take possession; have no home but in the holiest of all.

2. "Christ loved the church, and gave himself for it, that he might sanctify it." He gave himself! Have you caught the force of that word? Because He would have no one else do it,

because none could do it; to sanctify His Church, He gave *himself* to do it. And so it is His own special beloved work to sanctify the Church He loved. Just accept Him to do it. He can and will make you holy that He may present you to himself glorious, without spot or wrinkle. Let that word *himself* live in you. The whole life and walk in the house of God is in His charge. Having a Great High Priest, let us draw near.

3. This entrance into the holiest of all—an ever-fresh and ever-deeper entrance—is, at the same time, an ever blessed resting in the Father's presence. Faith in the blood, following in the way of the rent flesh, and fellowship with the living Jesus are the three chief steps.

4. Enter into the holiest of all and dwell there. It will enter into you, and transform you, and dwell in you. And your heart will be the holiest of all, in which He dwells.

5. Have we not at times been lifted by an effort of thought and will, or in the fellowship of the saints, into what seemed the holiest of all, but suddenly have felt that the flesh had entered there too? It was because we entered not by the new way of life—the way through death to life, the way of the rent veil of the flesh. O our crucified Lord! teach us what this means; give it us; be it yourself to us.

6. Let me remember that my access into the holiest is as a priest. Let me dwell before the Lord all the day as an intercessor, offering unceasing pleadings which are acceptable in Christ. May God's Church be like her of whom it is written, "She departed not from the temple, but served God with fastings and prayers night and day." It is for this that we have access to the holiest of all.

CHAPTER TWENTY-NINE

Holiness and Chastisement

"He [chasteneth us] for our profit, that we may be partakers of his holiness. Follow . . . holiness, without which no man shall see the Lord" (Heb. 12:10, 14).

Perhaps no part of God's Word sheds such divine light upon suffering as the Epistle to the Hebrews. It does this because it teaches us what suffering was to the Son of God. It perfected His humanity. It so fitted Him for His work as the compassionate High Priest. It proved that He who had fulfilled God's will in suffering obedience was indeed worthy to be its executor in glory, and to sit down on the right hand of the Majesty on high. "It became [God] . . . in bringing many sons unto glory, to make the author of their salvation perfect through sufferings." "Though he were a Son, yet learned he obedience by the things which he suffered, and being made perfect, he became the author of eternal salvation unto all them that obey him." As He said himself about His suffering, "I sanctify myself," so we see here that His sufferings were indeed to Him the pathway to perfection and holiness.

What Christ was and won was all for us. The power which suffering was proved to have in Him to work out perfection, the power which He imparted to it in sanctifying himself through suffering, is the power of the new life that comes from Him to us. In the light of His example we can see and in the faith of His power we too can prove that suffering is

189

to God's child the token of the Father's love, and the channel of His richest blessing. To such faith the apparent mystery of suffering is seen to be nothing but a divine need—the light affliction that works out—yea, *works out* and actually effects the exceeding weight of glory. We agree not only to what is written, "It became him . . . to make the author of salvation perfect through sufferings," but we understand somewhat how divinely fitting and right it is that we too should be sanctified by suffering.

"He [chasteneth us] for our profit, that we may be partakers of his holiness." Of all the precious words Holy Scripture has for the sorrowful, there is hardly one equal to this in leading us more directly and more deeply into the fullness of blessing that suffering is meant to bring. It is His holiness, God's own holiness, of which we are to partake. The epistle had explained clearly about our sanctification from its divine side, as worked out for us, and to be formed in us by Jesus himself. "He which sanctifieth and they which are sanctified are all of one." "We have been sanctified by the one offering of Christ." In our text we have the other side, the progressive work by which we are to accept personally, and voluntarily appropriate this divine holiness. What is this progressive work? There is much in us that clashes with God's will and that must be discovered and broken down before we understand what it is to give up our will and delight in God's. Only a personal experience and fellowship of suffering can lead to the full appreciation of what Jesus bore and did for us. Also, there must be the full personal entrance into the satisfaction with the love of God as our sufficient portion. Seeing these things, it is clear that chastisement and suffering are indispensable elements in God's work of making holy. In these three aspects we shall see how what the Son needed is what we need, how what was of such unspeakable value to the Son will be no less rich to us in blessing.

Chastisement leads to the acceptance of God's will. We have seen how God's will is our sanctification; how it is in the will of God Christ has sanctified us; yea more, how He found the power to sanctify us in sanctifying himself by the entire surrender of His will to God. His "I delight to do thy will" derived its value from His continual "Not my will." Where God comes with chastisement or suffering, His first object is to ask for and accomplish in us union with His own blessed will, that through it we may have union with Him and His love. He chooses one single point in which His will crosses our most cherished affection or desire, and asks the surrender of what we will to what He wills. When this is done willingly and lovingly, He leads us on to see how that individual sacrifice is based on a principle—that in everything His will is to be our one desire. Happy is the soul to whom affliction is not a series of single acts—of conflict and then submission to His will—but an entrance into the school where we prove and approve all the good, perfect and acceptable will of God.

Sometimes, even to God's children, it appears that affliction is not a blessing. It so arouses the evil nature and calls forth all the opposition of the heart against God's will that it has brought loss of the peace and the piety that once appeared to reign. Even in such cases the affliction is working out God's purpose. "That he might humble thee, to prove thee, to know what was in thine heart," is still His object in leading into the wilderness. To an extent we are not aware of, our religion is often selfish and superficial. When we accept the teaching of chastisement in unmasking the self-will and love of the world which still prevails, we have learned one of its first and most needful lessons.

This lesson is especially difficult when the trial does not come direct from God, but through men or circumstances. In looking at second causes and in seeking for their removal, in the feeling of indignation or grief, we often entirely forget to see God's will in everything His providence allows. As long as we do so, the chastisement is fruitless, and perhaps only hardens the more.

If, in our study of the pathway of holiness, there has been awakened in us the desire to accept, and adore, and stand complete in all the will of God, let us first seek to recognize that will in everything that comes to or upon us. The sin of the one who vexes us is not God's will. But it is God's will that we should be in that position of difficulty to be tried and tested. Let our first thoughts be: "This position of difficulty is my Father's will for me. I accept that will as my place now where He sees fit to try me." Such acceptance of the trial is the way to turn it into blessing. It will lead on to an understanding and ever more constant abiding in all the will of God.

Chastisement leads to the fellowship of God's Son. The will of God outside of Christ is a law we cannot fulfill. The will of God in Christ is a life that fills us. He came in the name of our fallen humanity and accepted all God's will as it rested on us, both in the demands of the law and in the consequences which sin had brought upon man. He gave himself entirely to God's will, whatever it cost Him. And so He paved a way for us through suffering, not only through it in the sense of getting past it and out of it, but because of it, leading us on into the love and glory of the Father. And it is in the power which Christ gives in fellowship with himself that we too can love the way of the cross, as the best and most blessed way to the crown. Scripture says that the will of God is our sanctification, and also that Christ is our sanctification. Only in Christ do we have the power to love and rejoice in the will of God. In Him we have the power. He became our sanctification once and for all time by delighting to do that will. He becomes our sanctification in personal experience by teaching us to delight to do that will. He learned to do it. He could not become perfect in doing it other than by suffering. In suffering He draws near. He makes our suffering the fellowship of His suffering, and in it makes himself—who was perfected through suffering—our sanctification.

All you suffering ones whom the Father is chastening, come and see Jesus suffering, giving up His will, being made perfect, sanctifying himself. His suffering is the secret of His holiness, of His glory, of His life. Will you not thank God for anything that can admit you into closer fellowship with your blessed Lord? Shall we not accept every trial, great or small, as the call of His love to be one with himself in living only for God's will. This is holiness—to be one with Jesus as He does the will of God, to abide in Jesus who was made perfect through suffering.

Chastisement leads to the enjoyment of God's love. Many a father has been surprised as he had his first experience of how a child, after being punished in love, began to cling to him even more tenderly than before. In the same way to those who live at a distance from their Father, the misery in this world appears to be the one thing that shakes their faith in God's love, where in reality it is just through suffering that His children learn to know the reality of that love. Chastening is distinctly a father's prerogative; it leads so directly to the admission that it was needed and that it was done in love. Also, it awakens so powerfully the longing for pardon and comfort and deliverance that, strange though this may seem, it does indeed become one of the surest guides into the deeper experience of the divine love. Chastening is the school in which the blessed lesson is learned that the will of God is all love, and that holiness is the fire of love, consuming that it may purify, destroying the dross only that it may assimilate into its own perfect purity all that yields itself to the wondrous change.

"We know and have believed the love which God hath in us. God is love: and he that abideth in love abideth in God, and God in him." Man's destiny is fellowship with God, and fellowship and mutual indwelling of love. It is only by faith that this love of God can be known. And faith can grow only by being exercised and thrive only under trial. When visible things fail, faith's energy is aroused to yield itself to be possessed by the invisible, by the divine. Chastisement is one of faith's chosen attendants, to nourish it and lead it deeper into the love of God. This is the new and living way, the way of the rent flesh in fellowship with Jesus leading up into the holiest of all. There it is seen how the justice that will not spare the child and the love that sustains and sanctifies it are both one in the holiness of God.

You chastened saints, who are so specially being led in the way that goes through the rent veil of the flesh, you have boldness to enter it. Draw near; come and dwell in the holiest of all. Make your abode in the holiest of all. There you are made partakers of His holiness. Chastisement is bringing your heart into unity with God's will, God's Son, God's love. Abide in God's will. Abide in God's Son. Abide in God's love. Dwell within the veil, in the holiest of all.

Prayer

Most Holy God! once again I bless you for the wondrous revelation of your holiness. Not only have I heard you say, "I

194

am holy," but you have invited me to fellowship with yourself: "Be holy, as I am holy." Blessed be your name! I have heard also: "I make holy," your word of promise, pledging your own power to work out the purpose of your love. I thank you for what you have revealed in your Son, in your Spirit, in your Word, of the path of holiness. But how shall I bless you for the lesson of this day, that there is not a loss or sorrow, not a pain or care, not a temptation or trial, but that your love also means it and makes it to be a help in working out the holiness of your people. Through each you draw to yourself that they may taste how, in accepting your will of love, there is blessing and deliverance.

Blessed Father, you know how often I have looked upon the circumstances and the difficulties of this life as hindrances. Now, in the light of your holy purpose to make us partakers of your holiness and in the light of your will and your love, let my circumstances and even the difficulties of this life be helps to me from now on. Let, above all, the path of your blessed Son—proving how suffering is the discipline of a Father's love, and surrender the secret of holiness, and sacrifice the entrance to the holiest of all—be so revealed that in the power of His Spirit and His grace that path may become mine. Let even chastening, even the slightest, be from your own hand, making me partaker of your holiness. Amen.

Personal Application

1. How wonderful is the revelation in the Epistle to the Hebrews of the holiness and the holy-making power of suffering as seen in the Son of God! "He learned obedience by the things which he suffered." "It became God to make the author of our salvation perfect through suffering, for both he that sanctifieth and they who are sanctified are all of one." "In that he himself hath suffered, he is able to succour." "We behold Jesus, because of the suffering of death, crowned with glory and honour." Suffering is the way of the rent veil, the new and living way Jesus walked in and opened for us. Let all sufferers study this. Let all who are "holy in Christ" here learn to know the Christ in whom they are holy, and the way in which He sanctified himself and sanctifies us.

2. If we begin by realizing the sympathy of Jesus with

us in our suffering, it will lead us on higher: sympathy with Jesus in His suffering, fellowship with Him to suffer even as He did.

3. Let suffering and holiness be inseparably linked, as in God's mind and in Christ's person, so in your life through the Spirit. "It became God to make him perfect through suffering; for both he that sanctifieth and they who are sanctified are all of one." Let every trial, small or great, be the touch of God's hand, laying hold on you, to lead you to holiness. Surrender yourself into that hand.

4. "Insomuch as ye are partakers of Christ's sufferings, rejoice; for the Spirit of glory and of God resteth on you."

CHAPTER THIRTY

The Unction from the Holy One

"And ye have an unction [anointing] from the Holy One, and ye know all things. But the anointing which ye received of him abideth in you, and ye need not that any one teach you; but as his anointing teacheth you concerning all things, and is true, and is no lie, and even as it taught you, ye shall abide in him" (1 John 2:20, 27).

In the revelation by Moses of God's holiness and His way of making holy, the priests, and especially the high priests, were the chief expression of God's holiness in man. In the priests themselves, the holy anointing oil was the one great symbol of the grace that made holy. Moses was to make a holy anointing oil: "And thou shalt take . . . of the anointing oil, and sprinkle it upon Aaron . . . and upon his sons . . . and he shall be hallowed . . . and his sons . . . with him. It shall be an holy anointing oil. Upon man's flesh shall it not be poured; neither shall ye make any other like it; it is holy, and it shall be holy unto you" (Ex. 29:21; 30:25–32). With this the priests, and especially the high priests, were to be anointed and consecrated. "He that is the high priest among his brethren, upon whose head the anointing oil was poured . . . neither shall he go out of the sanctuary, nor profane the sanctuary of his God; for the crown of the anointing oil of his God is upon him" (Lev. 21:10, 12). And even so it is said of David, as type of the Messiah, "Our king is of the Holy One of Israel. I have found David, my servant; with my holy oil have I anointed him."

We know how the Hebrew name *Messiah*, and the Greek *Christ*, has reference to this. In the passage just quoted, the Hebrew is, "With my holy oil I have messiahed him." And so in a passage like Acts 10:38: "God *christed* Jesus of Nazareth with the Holy Ghost and with power. . . ." Ps. 45:7, "God hath messiahed thee with the oil of gladness above thy fellows." Heb. 1:9, "Thy God hath christed thee with the oil of gladness. . . ." And so we are called Christians,* because we are fellow partakers with Him of His christing, His anointing. This is the anointing of which John speaks, the chrisma or christing of the Holy One. The Holy Spirit is the holy anointing which every believer receives. What God did to His Son to make Him the Christ, He does to me to make me a Christian. "Ye have the anointing of the Holy One."

1. *You* have an anointing from the Holy One. It is as the Holy One that the Father gives the anointing. That with which He anoints is called the oil of holiness, the Holy Spirit. Holiness is indeed a divine ointment. Just as there is nothing so subtle and penetrating as the odor with which the ointment fills a house, so holiness is an indescribable, all-pervading breath of heavenliness which pervades the man on whom the anointing rests. Holiness does not consist in certain actions: this is righteousness. Holiness is the unseen and yet manifest presence of the Holy One resting on His anointed. Only direct from the Holy One is the anointing received, or rather, only in the abiding fellowship with Him in Christ, who is the Holy One of God.

Who receives it? Only he who has given himself completely to be holy as God is holy. The priest, who was separated to be holy to the Lord, received the anointing; upon other men's flesh it was not to be poured. How many would gladly have the precious ointment for the sake of its perfume to themselves! But only he who is wholly consecrated to the service of the Holy One, to the work of the sanctuary, may receive it. If anyone had said: "I would be glad to have the anointing, but not be made a priest; I am not ready to go and always to be at the call of sinners seeking their God," then he could have no share in it. Holiness is the energy that only

---

*As one of our Reformed Catechisms, *The Heidelberg*, has it, in answer to the question, Why art thou called a Christian?

lives to make holy, and to bless in so doing. The anointing
of the Holy One is for the priest, the servant of God Most
High. Only in the intensity of a soul truly roused and given
up to God's glory, God's kingdom, God's work, does holiness
become a reality. The holy garments were prepared only for
priests and their service. In all our seeking after holiness,
let us remember this. As we beware of the error of thinking
that work for Christ will make one holy, let us also watch
against the other error, the straining after holiness without
work. The priest who is set apart for the service of the holy
place and the Holy One and the believer who is ready to live
and die that the holiness of God may triumph among men
around him are the ones who will receive the anointing.

2. "The anointing teacheth you." The new man is created
in knowledge, as well as in righteousness and holiness. Christ
is made to us wisdom, as well as righteousness and sanctification. God's service and our holiness are above all to be a
free and full, an intelligent and most willing, approval of His
blessed will. And so the anointing, to fit us for the service of
the sanctuary, teaches us to know all things. Just as the
perfume of the ointment is a subtle essence, not visible or
tangible, only perceptible by smell, so the spiritual faculty
which the anointing gives is the most subtle there can be. It
makes "quick of scent in the fear of the Lord." It teaches us
by a divine instinct, by which the anointed one recognizes
what has the heavenly fragrance in it, and what is of earth.
It is the anointing that makes the Word and the name of
Jesus in the Word to be indeed as ointment poured forth.

Thus, the great mark of the anointing is teachableness.
It is the great mark of Christ, the Holy One of God, the
Anointed One, that He listens: "I speak not of myself; as I
hear, so I speak." And so it is of the Holy Spirit too: "He shall
not speak out of himself: whatsoever he shall hear, that shall
he speak." It cannot be otherwise: one anointed with the
anointing of this Christ, with this Holy Spirit, will be teachable, will listen so he can be taught. "The anointing teacheth." "And ye need not that any one teach you: but the
anointing teacheth you concerning all things." "They shall
be all taught of God" includes every believer. The secret of
true holiness is a very direct and personal relation to the
Holy One. All the teaching through the Word or men is made

entirely dependent on and subordinate to the personal teaching of the Holy Ghost. The teaching comes through the anointing. Not, in the first place, in the thoughts or feelings, but in that all-pervading fragrance which comes from the fresh oil having penetrated the whole inner man.

3. "And the anointing abideth in you." *In you.* In the spiritual life it is of deep importance always to maintain the harmony between the objective and the subjective: God in Christ above me, God in the Spirit within me. In us, not as in a locality, but in us, as one with us, entering into the most secret part of our being and pervading all, dwelling in our very body, the anointing abideth in us, forming part of our essential being. And this is only to the degree that we know it and yield ourselves to it, as we wait and are quiet to let the secret fragrance permeate our whole being. And this will be, not an interrupted, broken experience but one that is continuous, unvarying. Above circumstances and feelings, "the anointing abideth." Not, indeed, as a fixed state or as something in our own possession; but, according to the law of the new life, in the dependence of faith on the Holy One, and in the fellowship of Jesus. "I am anointed with fresh oil"—this is the objective side. Every morning the believer waits for the renewal of the divine gift from the Father. "The anointing abideth in you"—this is the subjective side. The holy life, the life of faith and fellowship, and anointing, is always, from moment to moment, a spiritual reality. The holy anointing oil, always fresh, the anointing abiding always, is the secret of holiness.

4. "And even as it taught you, ye abide in him." Here we have again the Holy Trinity: the Holy One, from whom the holy anointing comes; the Holy Spirit, who is himself the anointing; and Christ, the Holy One of God, in whom the anointing teaches us to abide. In Christ the unseen holiness of God was set before us, and brought near; it became human, vested in a human nature, that it might be communicated to us. Within us dwells and works the Holy Spirit, drawing us out to the Christ of God, uniting us in heart and will to Him, revealing Him, forming Him within us, so that His likeness and mind are embodied in us. It is thus we abide in Christ: the holy anointing of the Holy One teaches this to us. It is this that is the test of the true anointing: abiding in

Christ, as He meant it, becomes truth in us. Here is the life of holiness as the Thrice Holy gives it: the Father, the first, the Holy One, making holy; the Son, the second, His Holy One, in whom we are; the Spirit, the third, who dwells in us, and through whom we abide in Christ, and Christ in us. Thus it is that the Thrice Holy makes us holy.

Let us study the divine anointing. It comes from the Holy One. There is no other like it. It is God's way of making us holy—His holy priests. It is God's way of making us partakers of holiness in Christ. The anointing, received of Him day by day, abiding in us, teaching us all things, especially teaching us to abide in Christ, must be on us every day. Its subtle, all-pervading power must go through our whole life. The odor of the ointment must fill the house. Blessed be God, it can do so! The anointing that abides makes the abiding in Christ a reality and a certainty. God himself, the Holy One, makes the abiding anointing a reality and a certainty too. To His holy name be the praise!

Prayer

O Holy One, I come to you now for the renewed anointing. O Father, this is the one gift your child may most surely count on—the gift of your Holy Spirit. Enable me now to sing, "Thou anointest my head"; "I am anointed with fresh oil."

I confess with shame that your Spirit has been sorely grieved and dishonored. How often the fleshly mind has usurped His place in your worship! How much the fleshly will has sought to do His work! O my Father, let your light shine through me to convince me deeply of this. Let your judgment come on all that there is of human willing and running.

Grant me, Blessed Father, according to the riches of your glory, to be strengthened now with might by your Spirit in the inner man. Strengthen my faith to believe in Christ for a full share in His anointing. Day by day teach me to wait for and receive the anointing with fresh oil!

Father, help me and all your children to see that for the abiding in Christ we need the abiding anointing. We would walk humbly, in the dependence of faith, counting upon the inner and ever-abiding anointing. Then may we be a sweet savor of Christ to all. Amen.

Personal Application

1. I think I know now the reason why at times we fail in the abiding. We think and read, we listen and pray, we try to believe and strive to look to Jesus only, and yet we fail. What was missing was this: "His anointing teacheth you; even as it taught you, ye abide in him"; so far, and no farther.

2. The washing always precedes the anointing: we cannot have the anointing if we fail in the cleansing. When cleansed and anointed we are fit for use.

3. Would you have the abiding anointing? Yield yourself wholly to be sanctified and made meet for the Master's use. Dwell in the holiest of all, in God's presence. Accept every chastisement as a fellowship in the way of the rent flesh. Be sure the anointing will flow in union with Jesus. "It is like the precious ointment upon the head of Aaron, that went down to the skirts of his garments."

4. The anointing is the divine eye salve, opening the eyes of the heart to know Jesus. So it teaches to abide in Him. I am sure most Christians have no conception of the danger and deceitfulness of a thought religion, with sweet and precious thoughts coming to us in books and preaching, and little power. The teaching of the Holy Spirit is in the heart first; man's teaching, in the mind. Let all our thinking ever lead us to cease from thought, and to open the heart and will to the Spirit to teach there in His own divine way, deeper than thought and feeling. Unseen, within the veil, the Holy Spirit abides. Be silent and still, believe and expect, and cling to Jesus.

5. Oh, that God would visit His Church and teach His children what it is to wait for, and receive, and walk in the full anointing, the anointing that abides and teaches to abide! Oh, that the truth of the personal leading of the Holy Spirit in every believer were restored in the Church! He is doing it; He will do it.

CHAPTER THIRTY-ONE

Holiness and Heaven

"Seeing then that all these things shall be dissolved, what manner of persons ought ye to be in all holy living and godliness?" (2 Pet. 3:11).

"Follow . . . holiness, without which no man shall see the Lord" (Heb. 12:14).

"He that is holy, let him be holy still. The grace of the Lord Jesus be with the saints [holy ones]. Amen" (Rev. 22:11, 21).

We are on our way to see God. We have been invited to meet the Holy One face to face. The infinite mystery of holiness, the glory of the invisible God, before which the seraphim veil their faces, is to be unveiled, to be revealed to us. And that not as a thing we are to look upon and to study. But we are to see the Thrice Holy One, the living God himself. God, the Holy One, will show himself to us. Oh, the infinite grace and the inconceivable blessedness—we are to see God.

All our schooling here in the life of holiness is simply the preparation for that meeting and that vision. We are to see God, the Holy One. "Blessed are the pure in heart, for they shall see God." "Follow . . . holiness, without which no man shall see the Lord." Since the time when God said to Israel, "Be ye holy, as I am holy," holiness has been revealed as the only meeting place between God and His people. To be holy was to be the common ground on which they were to stand with Him. Holiness was the one attribute in which they were to be like God. To be holy was the one thing that was to prepare them for the glorious time when He would no longer need to keep them away, but would admit them to the full fellowship of His glory, to have the word fulfilled in them: "He that is holy, let him be made yet more holy."

In his second epistle, Peter reminds believers that the coming of the day of the Lord is to be preceded and accompanied by the most tremendous catastrophe—the dissolution of the heavens and the earth. He pleads with them to give diligence that they may be found without spot and blameless in His sight. He asks them to think seriously about what that coming day of the Lord will be and will bring to consider what the life of those who look for such things ought to be: "What manner of person ought ye to be in all holy living and godliness?" Holiness must be the one, the universal characteristic. At the close of our meditations on God's call to holiness and in the light of all that God has revealed of His holiness, and all that waits still to be revealed, we ask ourselves Peter's question, "What manner of persons ought ye to be in all holy living and godliness?"

Note first the meaning of the question. In the original Greek, the words living and godliness are plural. Alford says, "In holy behaviours and pieties; the plurals mark the holy behavior and piety in all its forms and examples." Peter would plead for a life of holiness pervading the whole man: our acts toward men and our worship and service toward God. True holiness cannot be found in anything less. Holiness must be the one, the universal characteristic of our Christian life. In God we have seen that holiness is the central attribute, the comprehensive expression for divine perfection, the attribute of all the attributes, the all-including term by which He himself, as Redeemer and Father, His Son and His Spirit, His day, His house, His law, His servants, His people, His name, are marked and known. Always and in everything, in judgment as in mercy, in His exaltation and His condescension, in His hiddenness and His revelation, always and in everything, God is the Holy One. And the Word would teach us that the reign of holiness, to be true and pleasing to God, must be supreme, must be in all holy living and godliness. There must not be a moment of the day nor a relation in life, there must be nothing in the outer conduct nor in the inmost recesses of the heart, there must be nothing belonging to us whether in worship or in business that is not holy. The holiness of Jesus, the holiness which comes of the Spirit's anointing, must cover and pervade all. Nothing, nothing may be excluded if we are to be holy. It must be as Peter said when he spoke of God's call—holy in all manner of living. It must be as he says here—"in all holy living and godliness." To use the significant language of the Holy Spirit, everything must be done "worthily of the holy ones," "as becometh holy ones" (Rom. 16:2; Eph. 5:3).

Note the force of the question. Peter says, "Wherefore, beloved, seeing that ye look for these things." We have been studying down through the course of Revelation the wonderful grace and patience with which God has made known and made partaker of His holiness, all in preparation for what is to come. We have heard God the Holy One calling us, pleading with us, commanding us to be holy as He is holy. We expect to meet Him, as to dwell through eternity in His light, holy as He is holy. It is not a dream. It is a living reality. We are looking forward to it as the only one thing that makes life worth living. We are looking forward to love to welcome us, as with the confidence of childlike love we come as His holy ones to cry, Holy Father!

We have learned to know Jesus, the Holy One of God, our sanctification. We are living in Him day by day, as those who are holy in Christ Jesus. We are drawing on His holiness without ceasing. We are walking in that will of God which He did and which He enables us to do. And we are looking forward to meeting Him with great joy, "when he shall come to be glorified in the holy ones, and to be admired in all them that believe." We have within us the Holy Spirit, the holiness of God in Christ come down to be a home within us, as the earnest of our inheritance. He, the Spirit of holiness, is secretly transforming us within, sanctifying our spirit, soul, and body, to be blameless at His coming. He is making us meet for the inheritance of the holy ones in light. We are looking forward to the time when He shall have completed His work, when the body of Christ shall be perfected, and the bride, all filled and streaming with the life and glory of the Spirit within her, shall be set with Him on His throne, even as He sat with the Father on His throne. We hope through eternity to worship and adore the mystery of the Thrice Holy One. Even here it fills our souls with trembling joy and wonder. When God's work of making holy is complete, how we shall join in the song, "Holy, holy, holy, Lord God Almighty, which wast, and art, and art to come!"

In preparation for all this the most wonderful events are to take place. The Lord Jesus himself is to appear. The power of sin and the world is to be destroyed. This visible system of things is to be broken up. The power of the Spirit is to triumph through all creation. There is to be a new heaven and a new earth, wherein dwelleth righteousness. Then holiness is to be unfolded in ever-growing blessedness and glory in the fellowship of the Thrice Holy: "He that is holy, let him be holy yet more." It is only necessary to ask the question for each believer to feel and acknowledge its force: "Wherefore, beloved, seeing that ye look for these things, what manner of persons ought ye to be in all holy living and godliness?"

"What manner of persons ought ye to be?" Is such a question needed? Can it be that God's holy ones—made holy in Christ Jesus, with the very spirit of holiness dwelling with them, on the way to meet the Holy One in His glory and love—can it be that they need the question? Alas! It was needed in the time of Peter; it is only too necessary in our day too. How sad there are so many Christians to whom the very word holy is strange and unintelligible, even though it be the name by which the Father in His New Testament loves to call His children more than any other. There are many Christians for whom the word holy has but little attraction because they have never seen that such a life is indeed possible—and unutterably blessed. It is sadder still how many there are, even workers in the Master's service, to whom the "all holy living and godliness" is yet a secret and a burden, because they have not yet consented to give up all, both their will and their work, for the Holy One to take and fill with His Holy Spirit. Again the cry comes from those who do know the power of a holy life, lamenting their unfaithfulness and unbelief, as they see how much richer their entrance into the holy life might have been and how much fuller the blessing they still feel so feeble to communicate to others. Peter's question is needed! Shall not each of us answer it by the Holy Spirit through whom it came?

Then we should pass it on to our brethren that we and they may help each other in faith, and live in joy and hope to give the answer our God would have.

Seeing that these things are, then, all to be dissolved, what manner of persons ought we to be in all holy living and godliness? The time is short. The world is passing away. The heathen are perishing. Christians are sleeping. Satan is active and mighty. God's holy ones are the hope of the Church and the world. It is they their Lord can use. What manner of persons shall we be in all holy living and godliness! Shall we not seek to be such as the Father commands, "Holy, as he is holy"? Shall we not yield ourselves afresh and undividedly to Him who is our sanctification, and to His Blessed Spirit, to make us holy in all our conduct and worship and service? Remembering the love of our Lord Jesus and the coming glory, in view of the coming end, of the need of the Church and the world, shall we not give ourselves to be holy as He is holy, that we may have power to bless each believer we meet with the message of what God will do? Then, together with them we may be a light and a blessing to this perishing world.

I close with the closing words of God's blessed Book, "He which testifieth these things saith, Yea, I come quickly. Amen: Come, Lord Jesus. The grace of the Lord Jesus be with the holy ones. Amen."

Prayer

Most Holy God! who has called us to be holy, we have heard your voice asking, What manner of persons ought we to be in all holy living and godliness? With our whole soul we answer in deep contrition and humility: Holy Father! we ought to be so different from what we have been. In faith and love, in zeal and devotion, in Christlike humility and holiness, O Father! we have not been before you and the world what we ought to be, what we could be. We pray now for all who unite with us in this prayer and implore you to grant a great revival of true holiness in us and in all your Church. We beseech you to visit all ministers of your Word, that in view of your coming they may take up and sound abroad the question, What manner of persons ought ye to be? Lay upon them and all your people such a burden about the surrounding unholiness and worldliness that they may not cease to cry to you. Grant them such a vision of the highway of holiness, the new and living way in Christ, that they may preach Christ our sanctification in the power and the joy of the Holy Ghost, with the confident and triumphant voice of witnesses who rejoice in what you do for them. O God, roll away the reproach of your people who, in spite of professing to be your people, have not been any humbler or holier, any more loving, or any more heavenly than others.

O Holy God! give yourself the answer to your question, and teach us and the world what manner of persons your people can be, in the day of your power, in the beauty of holiness. We bow our knees to you, O Father, and ask that you grant us, according to the riches of your glory, to be mightily strengthened in the inner man by the Spirit of holiness. Amen.

Personal Application

1. What manner of men ought you to be in all the holy living? This is a question God has written down for us. Might it not help us if we were to write down the answer and say how holy we think we ought to be? The clearer and more distinct our views are of what God wishes, of what He has made possible, of what in reality ought to be, the more definite our acts of confession, of surrender, and of faith can become.

2. Let every believer, who longs to be holy, join in the daily prayer that God would visit His people with a great outpouring of the Spirit of holiness. Pray without ceasing that every believer may live as a holy one.

3. "Seeing that ye look for these things." Our life depends, in more than one sense, upon what we look at. "We look not at the things which are seen." It is only as we look at the invisible and spiritual, and come under its power, that we shall be what we ought to be in all holy living and godliness.

4. *Holy in Christ.* Let this be our parting word. However strong the branch becomes, however far away it reaches round the home, out of sight of the vine, all its beauty and all its fruitfulness ever depend upon that one point of contact where

it grows out of the vine. So be it with us too. All the outer circumference of my life has its center in the ego—the living, conscious I myself, in which my being roots. And this I is rooted in Christ. Down in the depths of my inner life, there is Christ holding, bearing, guiding, quickening me into holiness and fruitfulness. In Him I am, In Him I will abide. His will and commands will I keep; His love and power will I trust. And I will daily seek to praise God that I am holy in Christ.